DISCARDED

First published 2010

ISBN 978 0 7110 3478 5

© Ian Allan Publishing Ltd 2010

Published by Ian Allan Publishing

an imprint of Ian Allan Publishing Ltd, Hersham, Surrey, KT12 4RG

Printed in England by Ian Allan Printing Ltd, Hersham, Surrey, KT12 4RG

Code: 1010/B3

Distributed in the United States of America and Canada by BookMasters Distribution Services

Visit the Ian Allan Publishing website at www.ianallanpublishing.com

Front cover: The remains of what looks like an STL surrounded by devastated cars and buildings after a raid on Portman Square, 19 September 1940. *Author's collection*

The mechanism working the floodgates at Charing Cross Underground station. *Author's collection*

For Clive Gillam

and those we cared for
who did not survive the war

Contents

Introduction

'What did you do in the war, Daddy?' my sons might have asked if they had not had better things to do, mostly concerned with what was to come rather than what had been. Had they done so I would probably have replied, 'Went on growing up.' This would not have been a facetious answer for that's what I did, being two years and two months old when war began, a month off eight years when my mother turned to me as we walked down Richmond Hill, Bournemouth on a sunny May afternoon in 1945 and said, 'Look, they're putting the flags out at the *Echo* offices, the war must be over,' and a couple of months older again when, back in Thornton Heath in our partially repaired house, my friend Derek and I set out to see who could draw the biggest explosion, atomic-bomb style. Derek's father was a fireman with the National Fire Service, an emergency, wartime organisation which used grey-painted machines, Austins, which looked rather like large delivery vans but sporting a proper fireman's ladder as opposed to the regular appliances which, to the best of my memory, remained red throughout the war, and very impressive they looked, with their crews sitting in the open air along the sides.

Five and a half years is an enormously long time in the life of a child and for me the war was the norm. In those five and a half years more people died – no-one knows precisely how many – than had ever died in any previous five and a half years in the history of our planet. So when I write that we, that is our family, friends, neighbours and schoolmates, got on with our lives, went for days out in the country by bus, or up to London by tram, swapped copies of the *Dandy* and *Beano*, envied those who by way of older brothers had access to proper O-gauge Hornby layouts or even, very rarely, Hornby Dublo sets, laughed at a very funny man whose name I cannot recall on the Home Service who impersonated a whole family of children, the sayings of the youngest of whom,

Horace, he had to have translated by the next one in seniority, and above all to the jovial incompetence of Kenneth Horne, Richard Murdoch, Sam Costa and Maurice Denham at RAF Much Binding in the Marsh, I don't make light of the fact that war is obscene and horrible.

War is also 'seductive', to quote J. G. Ballard. Whilst I was being educated by Mrs Edwards, who would sometimes refer to her Eighth Army son who had been captured by the Germans in the North African desert, Ballard, almost the same age as me, was being held in a Japanese Prisoner of War camp. By 'seductive' I take it to mean that, terrified as I was to be fetched from my bed in the night and sat with the rest of the family under the stairs, where we could hear the thump of bombs falling, or in the Anderson shelter at the end of the garden where we couldn't, I was hardly unique in being fascinated by the re-creation in the Fairfield car park of a Burmese jungle or the interior of a Wellington bomber, or being delighted on Christmas Day, 1944 to find at the end of my bed a model of a de Havilland Mosquito – 'the fastest fighter/bomber in the RAF'.

The jokey silliness of Much Binding in the Marsh was a necessary antidote to stories in the paper of remarkable survivals of damaged Lancaster bombers which their crews had somehow managed to bring home from a raid over Germany. The Battle of Britain was fought over my head, largely by Hawker Hurricanes, although Supermarine Spitfires seemed to attract most of the retrospective glory, the nearest Fighter Command aerodrome being the former London Airport at Croydon, within walking distance of home, with Kenley and the most famous of all, Biggin Hill, each a bus ride away. I suppose had I been let out of the house by my parents I might have been machine-gunned by an Me109 – such things did happen – but I wasn't, and when I did venture out when the fighting seemed to be over for the time being I was warned not to touch shrapnel, for it

Thornton Heath depot, where the author spent many happy hours watching the inspector pulling the points lever which directed local route 42 up Brigstock Road. Many pointsmen would have been out in all weathers, such as the rain which has just ceased to fall, but here he has been provided with a hut, still labelled 'C.C.T.' (Croydon Corporation Tramways), although the picture was taken well into London Transport days. The building behind, which always struck the author as forbiddingly Dickensian and gloomy, had been the headquarters of the Corporation tramways department. Few tears can have been shed when it was demolished in February 1950, along with the depot, in readiness for the building of the replacement bus garage. *Ian Allan Library*

might still be red-hot. Of course, if you were outside during a raid you might well be struck, and almost certainly killed, by a piece of shrapnel which was more likely to be the exploded fragments of a British anti-aircraft shell than anything else: so-called 'friendly fire'. Was there ever a greater misnomer? Some eight years later, as a very raw trainee reporter on the *Croydon Advertiser* I was sent to interview a National Service infantryman, on leave from serving in Korea where he had been mentioned in despatches for rescuing a comrade who had been wounded by 'friendly fire'. He refused to talk about his experiences. I should, of course, have persisted, but instead I sat in his lounge, looking at him and thinking: 'By what right do I, an inexperienced 16-year-old youth who wasn't even much keen on being a Boy Scout, have to question the unimaginable experiences this man has been through?'

A near miss by a flying bomb, a V1, necessitated our removal in the late summer of 1944 to Bournemouth, and on cloudless days I would see high against the clear blue sky a patchwork of vapour trails as the bomber squadrons assembled before heading out over the English Channel. Even then I wondered how they managed not to collide with each other as they climbed, hundreds of them, almost wing-tip to wing-tip, into formation. In fact they often did collide. A good 20% of bomber crew losses were through collisions. Many of these would

have been USAF Flying Fortresses. Beneath them Bournemouth was awash with American soldiers who were only too happy to talk to children. Although to me they were all grown men, many of them must have still been in their teens and too young to have children of their own. For me to meet a real live American was quite something, for until then I had only come across such exotic creatures in shades of grey on the cinema screen.

Did I fear dying or that we would lose the war? I suppose I must have considered the first eventuality, although only remotely, for I did not personally know of any school friend who had died in an air raid. I did worry about catching polio, a real scourge of the 1930s and '40s, which happened to Brian across the road who recovered but who ever afterwards walked with a very bad limp and couldn't play any sports. My only relation who died in the war was Cousin Fred, about the same age as the young American GIs I used to talk to on the cliff paths at Bournemouth. I have such a clear memory of the last time I saw him, standing in front of the fireplace in his terrace house at 17, Addington Road, Croydon, throwing his older daughter, Ellen in the air. Fred was killed during the D-Day landings leaving his wife, Joan, aged 23 and my second cousins, Billy, Ellen and Betty.

As for losing the war – well, I knew this could not happen, for I caught a reference on a radio programme to 'German civilians keeping their best

Right: An early gas-producer experiment; the trailer, which is being filled with anthracite, is attached to Country Area ST132 at Chiswick Works on 16 November 1939.
London Transport Museum

clothes to celebrate victory'. I asked my mother how this could be, as I knew we were going to win, and she replied 'Of course we are,' which settled the matter entirely to my satisfaction.

Wellington and Lancaster bombers might have been exotic weapons of war seen only on Movietone news or in newspaper pictures, but convoys of tanks and Bren-gun carriers, the latter a particular favourite of mine, frequently passed by the top of our road and probably were regarded as something of a nuisance by ordinary road users. I certainly recall seeing such a column being passed on the main London Road at Norbury by a Croydon-bound ST which was being driven furiously, weaving in and out of the armoured vehicles. My father, who had been a driver in World War 1 and a chauffeur after that, bought a Lanchester 10 for £3 10s from a dealer on Brixton Hill in 1942, and on our first seaside holiday in it in 1946 – using precious petrol coupons – we got stuck behind a military convoy on the narrow, winding road which crossed the Romney Marshes and it seemed to take for ever to get from Rye to Hythe.

Lanchester, a long-vanished make, was owned by Daimler. Dad had been trained by Daimler before World War 1, and spoke lovingly of the sophistication of the patent Daimler fluid flywheel which our Lanchester also possessed. Dad explained that it enabled you to select a gear but that you only changed up, or down, to it when you were ready. I thought this highly sophisticated, although I wasn't quite sure why. The London RT was also equipped with this feature and if you sit immediately behind the driver on a preserved example you can see how it works. Daimler buses passed the end of our road although, being of wartime origin, not even Daimler would have accused them of being sophisticated.

A number of the 48-seat, LGOC-designed double-deck STs were singled out during the war for the indignity of conversion to gas as a fuel in order to save petrol. Croydon, being stocked with STs, equipped some which passed the top of our road on the 59A, as well as the 197 which ran from Norwood

Junction to Caterham Valley. The power generated by producer gas was much less than that by normal means and so routes which involved little or no hills were chosen. Hopefully no gas-producer 197 was ever diverted by the route which the 409 took out of Caterham Valley on its way to Croydon, for it involved a ferocious climb past a fetching and appropriate Swiss style chalet halfway up the Alpine-like ascent. The gas was generated in a two-wheel trailer towed behind the bus which the late transport historian John Price vividly described as 'resembling a hot-chestnut machine'. We had a horse-chestnut tree in our garden, not that it ever produced any fruit, but the edible variety were plentiful in the district, and we baked these ourselves.

In 2006, I had the good fortune to interview the remarkable 99-year-old Jack Lemmer, an engineer who had begun his career with the London General Omnibus Company in 1923. Called up with a commission in the REME in 1939, after only a week he was summoned to the office of Government minister and distinguished scientist Sir Harold Hartley MC, who said to him, 'I want you to come out of the army and work on using producer gas for London buses.' Jack said his wife was rather disappointed, as 'she liked me in uniform'. He went back to Chiswick and took charge of the gas-producer programme for the rest of the war. Not the least of the problems was that if the gas, which was produced by burning anthracite, was running low, the trailer more likely than not would produce flames. My father, who was an air-raid warden throughout the Blitz, and his comrades would not have taken kindly to a bus towing a bonfire behind it. Fortunately the gas-producer STs did not start work until the summer of 1943, which was just as well for by then air raids were much less of a threat.

I never saw a gas trailer on fire, but one morning stationed at my favourite post beside the inspector who worked the points at Thornton Heath Pond

Below: A military and civil-defence parade — such events were becoming much more familiar after the Munich crisis — brings the traffic to a halt at West Croydon in the autumn of 1938. An 'E1' tram, not yet fitted with a windscreen, is working local route 42 whilst ahead of it is a 'Feltham' bound for the Embankment. A Country Area forward-entrance STL is just setting out on its long journey from West Croydon on route 409 to Forest Row, on the edge of the Ashdown Forest. *Author's collection*

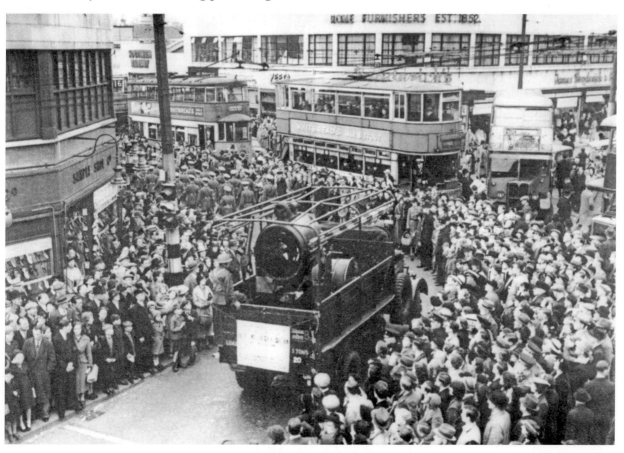

7

A column of troops 'somewhere in a Surrey village', a few days before D-Day, with a Bren-gun carrier prominent. *Author's collection*

whilst my mother was shopping for her 'divi' in the Co-op opposite, I did see an 'E1' tram towed in by another to the depot, the towee severely blackened by fire which might have been the result of an air raid or merely an electrical mishap. I travelled a lot by tram and found a picture of a line of them severely knocked about in an air raid, the leading vehicles with the upper decks completely smashed, which was upsetting; just as I had nightmares about shopping arcades catching fire. Allders, one of Croydon's three large department stores, had an arcade through which we regularly passed; it suffered several direct hits during the Blitz. It survived, however, and is still flourishing today.

Whenever I ventured to the end of the 16/18 route at Purley a highlight was to peer into the depot from the upper deck of the 'Feltham' in which we were travelling and catch a glimpse of some of the bedraggled, derelict 'E1s' ensconced therein. Again it was difficult to be sure whether their state was a result of enemy action or years of neglect. Mention of the 'Felthams' gives one pause to consider that, but for the war, I might never have had such clear and happy memories of riding these magnificent trams. Despite the fact that the 'Felthams' were light years ahead of

anything else which ran on rails in the streets of London and its suburbs — with perhaps the exception of the LCC's No 1, and even this (in which I travelled but once), although excellent, lacked the sheer, overwhelming presence of a 'Feltham' — the intention was that trolleybuses should totally replace trams by the mid-1940s. Of course, I cannot pretend to be unbiased, and I have to admit that when after the war I made the acquaintance of Liverpool's 'Liners' and 'Baby Grands' and Glasgow's 'Coronations' these certainly gave the 'Felthams' a run for their money. Trolleybuses were all right, and whilst exiled in Bournemouth I travelled to and from school each day on one, but nothing could equal the thrill of setting out for a day in London with my mother, or perhaps Great Aunt Hatt on a visit from Shropshire, patiently indulging my insistence that we let the lesser varieties of 'E1' or 'E3' go on their way until a 'Feltham' hove into view; then the climb up the long, straight staircase, to gain a seat at the very front of the upper deck, from which I had a grandstand view of all the exotic delights that Streatham, Brixton and Kennington, to say nothing of Waterloo station, Big Ben and Westminster, had to offer.

1

Evacuations and false alarms

London Transport had been in existence a little over six years when war broke out on 3 September 1939. It had been created on 1 July 1933, exactly two weeks before Adolf Hitler declared Germany to be a one-party state and had set in motion the process which would inexorably lead to World War 2, even if at that time he hoped that Britain would join him in an Aryan alliance and turn a blind eye to his plans for world domination. However much those who, recalling the horrors of World War 1 less than two decades distant, hoped that war could be avoided, the reality was that it could not. London Transport, whilst setting in motion far-reaching schemes for modernisation of every aspect of public transport in the capital and the 2,000 square miles out into the Home Counties for which it was responsible, at the same time prepared for war.

Many expected an aerial bombardment on such a scale that London would be virtually wiped out. The Alexander Korda film *Things to Come*, released in 1936, and based on an H. G. Wells story, had given a grim prediction of this. Ralph Richardson played a Mussolini-type character, thus ensuring the film would not be seen in Italy, Raymond Massey an heroic one. Unrelenting in its depiction of the destruction wrought on the imaginary Everytown, many took this as a prediction of what would happen to London, with thousands, if not millions, killed or wounded within the first few days of the declaration of war.

I have a clear memory of the day war was declared. My parents had taken me to Richmond for a day out on the river. It was sunny and warm, on 3 September 1939, still summer, and I was sitting in my push-chair on the station about to set off home when I became aware that something untoward and upsetting was going on. Air-raid sirens were sounding, a horrible noise with which we would become only too familiar in the years to come. There must have been a fair

War is declared, London, 3 September 1939. A corporal is on the far left, with two STLs in the background. *Author's collection*

A policeman on a cycle blows a whistle and warns of an air raid on 3 September 1939, the day war was declared. In the background is ST212, with an STL on route 11 behind. The two drivers, hurrying into action, are both still wearing summer uniform. Very quickly much more sophisticated methods of warning of air raids would come into use, and once air raids had become the norm drivers would decide for themselves whether or not to take cover.
London Transport Museum

amount of panic on what would have been a crowded station, although I have no recall of this and no doubt my parents — my father had seen plenty of action in the Middle East in World War 1 — would have reassured me. More than this I cannot recall, although I have no doubt that it was Richmond station, for its walls were smooth and white and rounded at the edges, made of concrete, and quite different to any wall I had ever encountered before. Whether this imbued in me a lasting love of art deco — the station had been rebuilt two years earlier in this style, much favoured by the Southern Railway — I cannot say. Perhaps, given the unpleasantness of the situation, it ought to have had the opposite effect.

Nearly 70 years later I was talking to Clive Gillam, with whom I used to go bus- and trolleybus-spotting in 1947/8, with whom I still keep in touch and who was visiting from his home in Australia. Upon mentioning these walls he replied, 'Ah yes, we visited my father up in Scotland at his naval base on the Clyde, just before the war began, and I was much taken by a stone wall, I loved the feel of it.' It's tricky trying to separate what one's earliest memories are from events one has later been told about, but I'm sure Clive and I are not mistaken, for the feel of a distinctive wall can only be a first-hand experience.

In the late 1990s I was visiting the local museum at Richmond and got talking to one of the attendants, who filled in the details of that day in September 1939. Bearing in mind the aerial bombardment expected any moment once Neville Chamberlain had declared war on Nazi Germany, the defence forces were naturally extremely twitchy and nervous. An unidentified aircraft had been detected coming in over the coast and it was naturally assumed this was the beginning of a raid. In the immediate area south-west of Richmond, Vickers had set up a number of aircraft factories, and a little while later it was discovered that the 'raider' was simply a British aircraft returning to its Vickers base after a test flight over the English Channel.

The links between Vickers and London buses would be many, not the least being the setting up of the London Bus Preservation Group's museum in 1972 in a former Vickers building where during the war much experimental work had been carried out, notably on the adjoining pond by Dr Barnes Wallis in perfecting his famous bouncing bomb.

My Richmond experience was hardly unique. On the opposite side of London the *Kentish Mercury*, which covered Deptford and Lewisham, reported that 'All manner of conflicting rumours were current following the air-raid warning — the third since the outbreak of war — which was received early on Wednesday morning.' The Ministry of Information announced that fighter aircraft had been despatched to the East Coast but contact had not been made with the enemy. 'On returning some of our aircraft were mistaken for enemy aircraft, which caused certain batteries to open fire. This accounts for the rumours of a heavy aerial engagement.' The paper added that, 'The all clear signal (around 9am) released a flood of traffic,

Above: Not all improvements and modernisations ended abruptly on the outbreak of war. This is King's Cross on 8 November 1939, with a new Underground ticket hall under construction. A trolleybus can be seen approaching down St Pancras Road, where the redundant tramlines are still *in situ* although partly obscured by the roadworks. *Ian Allan Library*

pedestrian and vehicular, and for some time buses, trams and trains were crowded to their utmost capacity. Many people who had comparatively short distances to traverse found it quicker and more convenient to walk to their places of business.' Peter Ustinov in his memoirs states that it was a flock of gannets 'without any discernable markings' which caused the air raid sirens to wail, but this might have been a bit of typical Ustinovian embroidery of mere fact.

Initially it seemed that the predictions of immediate all-out war were going to be fulfilled. Within hours, the British liner *Athenia* was sunk in the Atlantic by a German U-boat and women and children being evacuated to the USA were drowned.

The war in the seas around Great Britain and Ireland had, indeed, begun, but the war in the air and on land did not reach Britain until the summer of 1940.

Some five months before the declaration of war, in the spring of 1939, a meeting had been held at the Ministry of Transport to finalise an evacuation plan. Although war had not yet become a reality, the plan was put into effect on 1 September and in four days some 1,218,000 people, around half of these schoolchildren and their teachers, had been moved out of London. The rest were expectant mothers, blind people, disabled children, the mentally handicapped and others. Some travelled all the way by bus or coach, the drivers being away for two days and sometimes getting no sleep for 36 hours. Most were taken by bus, tram, trolleybus or coach to 129 'entraining stations', the majority of them in the suburbs to avoid too much congestion at the main-line termini. London Transport provided 4,985 buses, 533 trams and 377 trolleybuses which brought evacuees to 72 Underground stations

Left: The Donaldson liner *Athenia*, sunk within hours of the declaration of war. Amongst its 1,103 passengers, travelling from Glasgow to Montreal, were many children being sent to Canada for safety. The sinking of the liner by submarine U30 with Captain Lemp in charge, without any warning, caused enormous outrage on both sides of the Atlantic; 300 of the passengers were American. One report talks of the disciplined British crew ensuring that all but 112 people survived, although a number of children died, but another account claims that some of the crew ransacked First Class cabins before taking to the boats. Germany was deeply embarrassed by the sinking and tried to claim that the *Athenia* was an armed merchantman, but no-one believed this. Four days later the captain of another U-boat, well aware of the *Athenia* incident, came across a UK-bound merchantman, the *Olivegrove*, fired a shot across her bows, allowed the crew to take to the lifeboats, torpedoed the ship but stayed alongside the lifeboats until an American rescue ship came into view, shook hands with the *Olivegrove*'s captain and departed. *Author's collection*

ANCHOR·DONALDSON LINE—Turbine Twin-Screw Steamship "ATHENIA"

whence they were taken further afield to main-line trains and their ultimate destinations. Ealing Broadway station, for example, handled over 100,000 extra passengers. Croydon, which would be one of the most heavily bombed areas, both during the Blitz in 1940/1 and during the flying bomb raids of 1944/5, evacuated 16,781 people including 14 homeless people (four mothers and 10 children). Interestingly, 27 of the evacuees went to Northern Ireland. By November 1940, some 50,000 people out of a population of around a quarter of a million had left Croydon and there were similar exoduses in many other boroughs, particularly to the east of Central London and south of the river.

The *Kentish Mercury* of 8 September 1939 reported that, 'As early as six o'clock on Friday morning there was a constant stream of buses and coaches along the Sidcup road which had been specially converted into a one-way road to cope with the outward flow of traffic and also to prevent congestion. The children still maintained that air of calmness which they had shown throughout the days prior to their evacuation. Accounts

Above: Girls of the Charles Edward Brooke School boarding 'HR2' tram No 120 in Camberwell New Road, on their way to Waterloo and evacuation on 1 September 1939. *London Transport Museum*

received from "Somewhere in the Country" show that the children are settling down and are, in fact, having a wonderful time.' The Paget family from Deptford, 'six little people, ages from three years to twelve years', found themselves in the extraordinary situation of being 'in a very big house and with a wealthy family'. When a reporter called to see how they were getting on he was informed 'by the butler that the master had taken them all in his car to the beach'.

Not all evacuees went far away from London. Ten-year-old Lionel Blue, now of course Rabbi Blue of Radio Four fame, 'went to a very nice little church school in Gerrards Cross, Buckinghamshire, where I learned to sing English songs which were much more cheerful than the Russian songs of my grandmother'. Gerrards Cross was well within London Transport territory, being served by several Country Area routes. He was brought back to the East End by his parents 'for the Blitz' as he wrote in typical Rabbi Blue style in the *Independent* on 14 May 2009. 'We all slept in the vaults of the brewery and had big sing-songs. The first thing we did in the morning was to see if our house was still there and then we went back to school. We had to go home during the air raid which was usually just after noon.'

Not everyone enjoyed being an evacuee. Experiences ranged from the ecstatically joyful to the utterly miserable. 'In Aylesbury,' (again somewhere within London Transport Country Area territory) reported Councillor Gough to a meeting of Croydon Council, 'there seemed to be a reluctance to receive evacuees. Householders were using all kinds of tricks to rid themselves of evacuees.' To be fair the Councillor added 'that he only mentioned that district because he had personal knowledge of the conditions there'. But it was not unique. Keswick landladies resented the fact that they were paid exactly half to keep an evacuee compared with what they could charge a holidaymaker, and one mother was told the only part of the house she could sit in was the kitchen.

Not all evacuees made a favourable first impression. The *Ilford Recorder* tells of two brothers, aged 12 and eight, in shorts and gym shoes, with grubby legs and shirts none too clean, an extra shirt and vest in a paper bag, arriving at a small, neat, terrace house. George hands the lady of the house 'a smudged scrap of paper, already well-thumbed by previous readers', from their father and she reads, "My advice to you is thrash George good and hearty. He's rough at home and rough at school. His mother and I don't mind how hard you lam into him." After a while, bored, they start running up and down the stairs and, shortly, there is a loud crash. The lady of the house finds the clock on the hall table knocked over, its glass shattered. She discovers the boys cowering behind the kitchen door. She approaches, clock in hand. "Would you boys like to go into the village this afternoon and see if Mr Brown, the carpenter, can give you a new piece of glass for it?" Silence. "You broke it, banging into it, didn't you? I shouldn't run up and down stairs so fast another time. But it was stupid of me to leave it on the table." George looks at her in surprise.

"Aren't you going to beat us?"

"No," said his hostess, "If I beat you it wouldn't stop this clock having been broken, would it?"

"We didn't mean to break your clock, we are sorry aren't we, Jim?"

"Sure, that's right, can we take the clock and get it put right?"

The following week the billeting office calls and finds the lads pasting brown paper over the hall windows. Their hostess tells the officer that she and her husband are going that night to a whist drive, leaving George to answer the telephone and Jimmy to clear away tea. They are going to continue doing the blackout. The billeting officer gapes and asks: "Do you mean to say you trust them?" The response is a laugh.

Some found themselves living deep in the countryside, taking part in rural activities, becoming familiar with farm animals they had at first been scarcely able to recognise, fed on fresh food — sometimes more than they had ever seen in their young lives — which they helped to harvest, and were welcomed with open arms into a warm, caring community. To an extent this was my experience. Although not officially evacuated when our house was badly damaged by a V1 'doodlebug' in 1944, we went to stay with my aunt and uncle in Shropshire, where Uncle Frank was cowman on a large farm and I spent day after day in the fields, riding on hay carts and the back of tractors (highly dangerous practices in retrospect), watching Uncle Frank milking a cow by hand, his cap turned back to front so he could press his head into the cow's flank as he pulled at her teats. He let me have a go, but I had little success in producing any milk, the cow turning her head to give me a hard stare, no doubt wondering who on earth had let loose this half-size incompetent.

Not everyone's experience of rural life was good. Wrenched from home and everything familiar, a child could find himself or herself billeted with people who took them in only for the money they brought, treated them as unpaid, half-starved servants and made their lives utterly miserable. Many evacuees had little contact with their parents and when they finally returned home after perhaps as much as four years, they were almost like strangers to each other. When the anticipated holocaust failed to materialise, many evacuees drifted back home and even when the Blitz began in earnest many families preferred to stay at home together. The *Croydon*

The author and his mother haymaking in Shropshire in the summer of 1944 after being bombed out of their house in Thornton Heath.
Author's collection

Advertiser on 19 October 1940 noted that, 'The Council in November last agreed to pay the rents for the rooms and houses … left by evacuated blind persons, then estimated at some £15 per week … The number of evacuated persons has steadily diminished, the rents payable … now amounting to £6 3s 10d per week.'

There were other types of evacuees, both in and out of London. In 1940 a number of provincial companies sent buses to help out in the capital, although, given that the number of buses actually needed was less than in peacetime, it is generally assumed that this was a gesture of solidarity rather than a necessity. A little later a number of London buses returned the compliment, by taking up work in towns and cities all over England, Wales and Scotland.

Despite the 'Phoney War', as it came to be known, continuing throughout the remainder of 1939 and into 1940, in France there were casualties, and the

Golders Green during the 'Phoney War', May 1940. Sandbags are in place, a Green Line 10T10 on the H1 heads along Golders Green Road on its way to Luton, passing a roofbox STL, as another STL swings into Finchley Road. Under the bridge, over which a Tube train is passing, a trolleybus heads northwards whilst another is approaching. An early LGOC-type T is in the bus station. *London Transport Museum*

directors of the London Passenger Transport Board was asked to consider the case of Driver T. J. Page, 'killed in an accident on 27 September 1939 whilst serving with the British Expeditionary Force in France'. In normal circumstances his widow would have received a grant of £35, but the Board decided to defer the matter until it had learned what provision the Government would make for dependants of servicemen killed whilst on duty. The Phoney War lulled many into a false sense of security, and it was estimated that almost a third of the evacuees had returned to London by early 1940.

2

Preparations
put into practice

On 1 September 1939 the blackout was imposed throughout Britain. I'm not sure whether the term had previously been in use but it has certainly permanently entered the English language. Parliament had passed the Emergency Powers (Defence) Act six days earlier which meant the Government could act in any way it felt necessary without getting the approval of Parliament. The blackout meant literally what it said. All street lighting was turned off, as, of course, were illuminated adverts, and no light was allowed to be shown from any window, whether it be commercial premises, such as shops, or private dwellings. My father, who had served as a driver throughout World War 1, was too old for this one but had become an Air Raid Warden and one of his principal duties was to check that blackout regulations were adhered to. 'Put that light out!' became something of a catchphrase, and although a few people got rather annoyed when the warden knocked on their front door and told them that a light was showing, the great majority understood the need for total darkness, particularly when the air raids on London began in the late summer of 1940.

Dad would go out with other wardens each night, whether there was an air raid or not. Mum and Granny must have worried greatly for him, I less so on account of being assured that he 'would be all right'. If there had been a raid, those bombed out would sometimes be brought back to our house. On one occasion which must have been at the very beginning of the Blitz, for I was actually carried down for breakfast, I found a crowd of people sitting around our big kitchen table drinking tea and coffee. At the far end was an ancient, rickety wickerwork chair covered in several equally ancient blankets, which was for the exclusive use of our dog, Trix. One of the refugees from the bombing was sitting in it and I called out, 'You can't sit there, that's the dog's chair.' I was somewhat taken aback when, instead of being instantly obeyed, there was laughter all round. I had presumably supplied a bit of much needed light relief.

All vehicles had to be fitted with an officially approved mask for both headlamps and sidelights. Initially too much light was found to be projected through the original headlamp mask, which was replaced. Vast amounts of white paint were applied to vehicle extremities, kerbs, platform edges, posts etc. All dashboard lights had to be disconnected. Interior lights on buses, trams, trolleybuses and trains were dimmed, initially in some instances by painting windows and bulbs blue, until a standard form of mask was devised. Cycles, probably the commonest of all means of transport at the time, were certainly not ignored. The Government gave strict instructions that 'during an air raid a cyclist must continue to use the regulation front and rear lights'.

The author's father in his ARP uniform. *Author's collection*

Without giving it much thought I used idly to wonder why the trams, unlike the motor buses and trolleybuses, retained their masks after the war and, indeed, until replaced by buses in the period 1950-2. The reason, apparently, was that the masks actually projected a brighter red light to the rear, presumably because it was more focused. This was at the expense of a less bright front light, but once full street lighting had been restored this was of no great import, no tram route ever operating in streets without lighting.

As might be imagined this sudden plunge into almost complete darkness after sunset caused many accidents. These mostly involved pedestrians being hit by vehicles which they had not seen. The *Hackney Gazette* in December 1940 reported that '19,545 civilians have been killed as the result of bombing since the Germans developed their air offensive on Britain. These (figures) compare with a total of 11,434 deaths on the road during the 15 months of war — an increase of no fewer than 3,141, or nearly 40% on the corresponding period immediately preceding the fateful September of last year.' When one considers that the death toll in the UK in 2008 on a much busier road network was 2,943 (which is actually the lowest figure since 1926), the figures of 70 years ago are truly shocking.

Local papers recorded many tragic accidents to pedestrians caused by the blackout. The *Croydon*

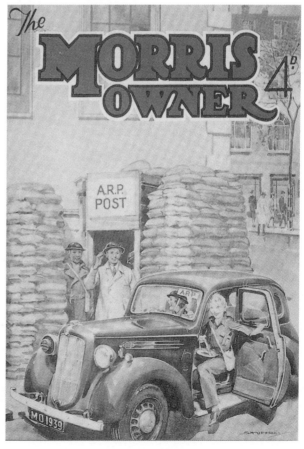

Right: A poster encouraging people at home to knit gloves and scarves for the RAF. It is impossible to identify the twin-engine aeroplane in the background, although the barrage balloon and its crew of three holding (in reality a winch would have been used) on to invisible ropes are clear enough. *Robert Opie collection*

Below: A London Transport fireman doing precisely as urged, knitting winter comforts for the troops, although in a year's time, at the height of the Blitz — this picture was taken in January 1940 — the firemen themselves could well do with protection from the cold and damp. Two of the firemen are sitting on the running board of the Chiswick Works fire engine, accompanied by one of the many cats which lived there. *London Transport Museum*

Advertiser of 2 November 1940 carried this headline: 'Sanderstead Man Killed In the Black-Out. Knocked Down by Bus on Way Home from Work.' William Smith, who had 'served throughout the Great War', was hit by a Country Area double-deck bus on the main Brighton Road just after 10pm. The bus driver, Mr M. W. Baynes of Redhill said, 'I was driving along the near side of the road, clear of the tram track, when a dark object suddenly loomed up in front of me in the darkness directly in front of my off-side headlamp. I jammed on both brakes as quickly as I could. I don't know whether I swerved or not. I did not even have time to think, it happened so quickly. The only lights on the bus were the regulation dimmed sidelights.' The conductor and driver got out and found the unfortunate man 'lying about three yards from the back of the bus, and on the tram track'. The conductor added, 'My driver picked up an overcoat from the road and laid it over Mr Smith … a tram conductor, whose tram had been following our bus, came up and called the ambulance. It was a wet, misty night, and there was no lighting in the road.' The Coroner, recording a verdict of 'Death by misadventure', concluded that 'There is no evidence at all that the driver of the bus was to blame. As is so common in blackout accidents there are, unfortunately, no independent witnesses.' It was not unknown for pedestrians on such dark, winter nights to walk along tram tracks to find their way and this might have been what the unfortunate William Smith was doing.

Around the same time the *Kentish Mercury* reported the death of a 73-year-old ARP worker, Henry William Rockliffe at Rushey Green. The conductor of a 36 bus, Harry Mawson of Downham said, 'It was a very dark night, and there was heavy gunfire overhead. The bus had a full load of passengers and was travelling very slowly.' The driver, Alfred Thomas Ralph of Hither Green, said his speed 'was about eight miles an hour' although buses did not have speedometers. Visibility was rather poor. About two feet in front of him he saw an object, and he swerved and applied both brakes. He was not quite certain what the object was, and when he switched on his headlights he found a man lying under the bus. The Deputy Medical Superintendent of Lewisham Hospital said the man was already dead when admitted there: 'I should think he was killed practically instantaneously by a blow on the head.' The Coroner recorded death from 'Accidental Causes', and the dead man's son said to him, having shaken hands with the bus driver, 'I do hope he will forget all this and that it will not affect his nerve in driving. I appreciate the strain under which these fellows work.'

Similar sentiments were expressed by Hackney's Deputy Coroner at the inquest into a Poplar woman who was run over by a trolleybus in the East India Dock Road during an air raid on 27 September 1940. The night 'was one of the darkest for some time' and the driver, approaching a request stop, was travelling at little more than walking pace. The Deputy Coroner remarked that 'it was amazing that bus drivers were involved in so few accidents during the blackout period'.

London Transport appreciated the extra strain put upon drivers by having to cope with blackout conditions and altered rotas so that this could be kept to a minimum. It was helped in this respect by the huge reduction in demand for services after dark.

Two London Transport employees whom, you might well consider, were treated with less sympathy, were a bus driver from Swanley and a tram driver of Camberwell. The bus driver, Frederick Charles Halford, was a witness to a traffic accident at New Eltham in November 1940 and asked if he could have a day's pay to attend the hearing. The exchange between Mr Halford and the Coroner as reported in the *Kentish Mercury* is worth repeating, albeit somewhat abridged.

Mr Halford: 'The Transport Board will not stand my day's loss of pay.'

Coroner: 'We are not employers of labour. When you come into the Court you are serving your country.'

Mr Halford: 'I can't afford to lose a day's pay.'

Coroner: 'I know you can't. It is for the employers to join with the workmen and see they get it.'

Mr Halford: 'That is no good to me, sir. They ask if an accident happens we must lay ourselves open to help the police but if this sort of thing is going to happen we might just as well close our eyes to it. I am only asking for my bare day's pay.'

Coroner: 'It seems strange that this should crop up with you only — other chaps have come here and got it.'

Mr Halford (growing impatient): 'Oh no they haven't.'

Halford said his day's pay was 17 shillings, two pence.

Coroner (growing equally impatient): 'And you think that every tram driver, every porter, every engine driver of the Transport Board can come to Court and claim 17 shillings and two pence?'

Mr Halford: 'I have been given to understand that that is so.'

Coroner (having the last word): 'I am afraid you have the wrong idea. It is perfectly absurd. The man in the street has to come along and accept the ordinary witness fee and to me you are only an ordinary man in the street.'

The tram driver was James Charles Brewer, of Camberwell. He was in charge of what was probably an 'E1' on the night of 28 July 1940 which crashed into another tram outside Lewisham Hospital just before midnight. Twenty-five people were injured, mainly from flying broken glass, including James Brewer himself. He was summoned at Greenwich Police Court 'for failing to bring his car to a standstill as soon as possible to avoid impending danger'. The conductor of the front tram was told there was an air-raid warning and he 'switched off the interior lighting, but left the platform lights on'. The driver of the second tram, James Brewer, said 'he did not see any lights on the tram in front. His car was lighted and he had received no intimation of an air-raid warning. This evidence was supported by a motor driver … who was a passenger in the defendant's car.' Despite this he was fined 3s plus costs of 17s 10d, which was almost exactly a day's pay.

It was around this time that it occurred to the police, and, presumably, to London Transport, that an unlit tram could very easily be stranded in the middle of the road, either through a bombing incident, or a breakdown or power failure, creating an additional hazard to those usually encountered during the blackout, and so modifications were quickly carried out on the entire fleet so that the headlamps, back and front, would remain lit from an emergency battery supply.

RT95 at the Putney terminus of route 14 shortly after entering service in May 1940. Both it and the roofbox STL are in full prewar red and white livery with silver roofs, although they have white blackout markings. The picture provides an interesting contrast between the two generations of standard double-deckers. *G. Robbins colllection*

In the midst of much tragedy and horror there was, however, still room for humour, if somewhat black in nature. In the same issue of the *Kentish Mercury* is a story headed 'Churchill caught in the Black-Out', subtitled 'So he lay on the Pavement for Safety'. It turns out that this Churchill was not — surprise, surprise — the Prime Minister, but one Edwin Churchill, a '70-year-old pensioner who has stood in the dock at Greenwich Police Court more times than any man living'. Caught in the blackout, Churchill said: 'Being pitch dark, I couldn't see my way back to the institution. I kept pushing into people and lamp-posts so I lay down on the pavement to get out of the danger. I suffer terribly from nerves owing to these air raids.' Sent to prison for a month, three years later he was still appearing in court, in June 1944 for the fourth Saturday in a row. He claimed that he couldn't possibly be the worse for drink, as 'I don't get enough to get drunk, I am suffering from debility and old age.'

In those days (indeed, until the end of the Routemaster era) London buses had open platforms — very handy for nipping on and off at traffic lights, but one does wonder how many accidents were caused by passengers' falling from them. And not just the rear open platform of double-deckers, for the Metropolitan Police insisted that single-deckers also have open entrances, usually at the front, and if they were fitted with doors these were to be permanently kept open. Early in 1941, during an air raid, a waiter, Ernest Bertram Green, was travelling on a Chislehurst-bound 228, presumably in an LT single-decker, when he fell. The conductor, Frank Edmeades of Bexley, said that there was an air raid in progress. Mr Green got up and went to the front of the bus. The conductor warned him that the bus was turning a corner. As the bus turned Mr. Green seemed to lose his balance. 'Witness made an effort to pull him back, but he fell from the platform into the road. When he went to him Mr Green was lying on the crown of the road on his back. He died 10 minutes after being admitted to hospital 'from, cerebral haemorrhage due to a fractured skull'.

3

Change of use

Fuel rationing began on 23 September 1939. London Transport had its diesel and petrol allocation reduced by 25%. Petrol supplies were the most heavily rationed and no fewer than 1,266 Central buses were withdrawn. The activities of the 48- seat ST class were heavily curtailed, all the Tilling variety being withdrawn. The standard forward-entrance Country Area STLs, which seated eight less than the standard rear-entrance buses, were also, temporarily, taken out of service, although they soon returned, being needed where a number of hitherto single-deck routes, which for various reasons found themselves much busier now, required double-deckers, and also because the armed services had more need of petrol than diesel.

The opportunity was also taken to remove from the active fleet the little 20-seat Dennis Darts and Bedfords and the final 30 members of the TD class. These latter were elderly petrol-engined Leyland Titans, absorbed into the fleet in 1933 from independents and in any

TD130, a Leyland Titan TD2 which entered service with the Prince Omnibus Co and was taken over by London Transport in 1933, working from Hanwell garage shortly before withdrawal in 1939. It saw further service with Red & White. *Author's collection*

case due for retirement. In the normal course of events they would have been scrapped but wartime exigencies meant that there was work elsewhere for them and many went off to the provinces, some far away to Liverpool and Cumberland.

One rather anachronistic feature of services in the Central Area in peacetime was the duplication of considerable sections of the road system by motor buses, trams and/or trolleybuses. There were also duplications of route numbers, but we'll put that aside for the moment. War conditions gave London Transport the opportunity to remove many of these, the motor-bus services, requiring petrol or diesel fuel, naturally enough being those identified. There were also instances where bus services were withdrawn if they were paralleled by an Underground line. However there were plenty of exceptions to this practice. The tram routes which passed the top of our road consisted of local number 42 and the 16 and 18, which ran between the Embankment and Purley. Between Thornton Heath Pond and Purley, a distance of some six miles, these routes shared the London Road with the 59 and 59B bus routes. These latter could easily have been curtailed to run just between Purley and Chipstead Valley and Old Coulsdon, their

respective southern termini; but they never were. One factor which might explain this was that allocations to routes were revised so that there was as little dead mileage as possible, as many routes as possible passing the garages which supplied the buses.

In contrast 19 express bus routes were introduced in October 1940. Those chosen were some of the principal trunk routes, running during the morning and evening rush hours. In this they anticipated the express routes of later decades. These were primarily to cover disruptions to the Underground network, although John Price has suggested that by decreasing running time fuel was saved. The outer-suburban part of the journey took in the regular stops, but then buses stopped only once, twice or three times before reaching their destination; for example the 25B, once it reached Ilford Broadway, stopped only at Stratford Broadway on its way to Aldgate, while the 159, on reaching Streatham station, stopped only at Telford Avenue, Brixton (Lambeth Town Hall — which

Two former London Titans find new owners far away with Cumberland. On the right is the former TD37, next to it the former TD27, whilst just visible on the left is ex-Southdown Titan UF 8383. *The Omnibus Society*

always used to confuse me as a child) and Thames House opposite Lambeth Bridge. The list is as follows:

9	Barnes–Hyde Park Corner
12	East Dulwich–Trafalgar Square
17	Shepherds Bush–Oxford Circus
21	Sidcup–London Bridge
23	Becontree Heath–Aldgate
25B	Becontree Heath–Aldgate (via Ilford)
29	Southgate–Trafalgar Square
35	Walthamstow–Liverpool Street
38	Chingford–Bloomsbury
47	Bromley–London Bridge
53A	Plumstead–Trafalgar Square
60	Colindale–Aldwych
76	Edmonton–Moorgate
77A	Raynes Park–Charing Cross
88	Mitcham–Charing Cross
113	Mill Hill–Oxford Circus
133	South Croydon–London Bridge
134	Friern Barnet–Victoria
159	Thornton Heath–Charing Cross

With much less traffic on the road than in peacetime the buses working these express routes must have been able to run at a steady 30mph for considerable distances.

Demand for London Transport's services after dark fell away dramatically, for the public was naturally wary of venturing out in such threatening conditions, even before the Luftwaffe began to take advantage of them from the summer of 1940.

Perhaps the most dramatic example was in the heart of London where the joint 2½min headway operated by routes 9 and 11 was reduced to a solitary number 11 every 20 minutes. Nevertheless, after initial shutdowns, theatres, cinemas, restaurants and nightclubs reopened and continued to offer entertainment well into the evening all through the war, so there remained a residual demand for public transport. There were many instances of bombs falling on places of entertainment but these did not deter those determined to enjoy themselves. After all, death was also lurking around the corner, and one might just as easily meet it in one's own home or place of work as out on the town.

One of the most famous entertainers to die in a bombing incident was Al Bowlly. The pop stars of the 1930s were generally band leaders such as Lew Stone, Henry Hall and Ambrose, but Bowlly was the exception. Brought up in South Africa, he was a consummate musician and by all accounts a charming character, his uniquely smooth and individual delivery lifting him clear of all other singers. He starred with Bing Crosby in the *Big Broadcast of 1936*, and although he made his last recording some 70 years ago his voice is still familiar today (even if few people recognise his name), for it has been used in countless TV productions and films, ranging from Denis Potter's *Pennies from Heaven*, which made a star of Bob Hoskins, to *Amelie* of 2001, which made a an international star of Audrey Tautou, and *Edge of Love* (2008), instantly evoking

A Tilling ST loading up with passengers at London Bridge before setting off on the express 47 service to Bromley. *Author's collection*

various London hospitals. Later many of the 10T10s found themselves enrolled into USA service. Some continued to serve as ambulances whilst the majority, 55, became Clubmobiles which meant being fitted out as mobile canteens with two beds for the operators who were members of the Red Cross. Nine other USA Red Cross vehicles served as transports.

The naming of the 10T10s was as follows:

T465 *South Dakota*	T650 *Kansas*
T479 *Maryland*	T652 *Seattle*
T510 *Wisconsin*	T654 *Florida*
T530 *Connecticut*	T656 *New Hampshire*
T535 *North Dakota*	T659 *Oklahoma*
T538 *Alabama*	T660 *Georgia*
T544 *Iowa*	T662 *Indiana*
T549 *Washington*	T665 *Rochester*
T551 *Utah*	T666 *Minnesota*
T561 *Tennessee*	T668 *Kansas City*
T565 *North Carolina*	T669 *Michigan*
T567 *Nebraska*	T673 *Buffalo*
T601 *Montana*	T674 *Baltimore*
T603 *Oregon*	T680 *Milwaukee*
T609 *South Carolina*	T682 *Illinois*
T612 *West Virginia*	T683 *Cincinnati*
T615 *Missouri*	T685 *Columbia*
T628 *Mississippi*	T689 *Minneapolis*
T630 *Pennsylvania*	T695 *New York*
T632 *Arkansas*	T696 *Kentucky*
T633 *Colorado*	T701 *Newark*
T635 *Rhode Island*	T702 *Maine*
T637 *New Orleans*	T703 *Ohio*
T639 *Louisiana*	T705 *San Francisco*
T640 *Texas*	T708 *Massachusetts*
T646 *New Jersey*	T710 *Boston*
T649 *California*	T712 *Houston*

A nurse smiles for the camera at the rear emergency door of a 10T10 ambulance. The inside of the door looks to have a poster showing how the stretchers should be loaded, an example of the preparations which had been going on for many months. *London Transport Museum*

the 1930s and the early 1940s. It is often stated that Bowlly died in the bombing of a West End nightclub; in fact his death occurred at his flat in Jermyn Street on 17 April 1941. He had just returned on the last train from High Wycombe, where he had been performing at the Rex Cinema and an incendiary bomb exploded outside his flat, the blast bringing about his death.

Green Line services ended abruptly on 31 August, and some 477 coaches were in the remarkably short time of two days converted to ambulances — yet more evidence of the detailed planning which London Transport had been working on for many months. Each coach was fitted out with eight or 10 stretchers and was used to transport patients from

The names must have been a bitter-sweet reminder of home for GIs. As a schoolboy in Bournemouth in 1944/5 I was fascinated by the thousands of American soldiers in the town, on their way to fight in France and Germany. They seemed like grown men to me but of course many would have still been in their teens, from a huge variety of backgrounds: country boys from the Mid-West, probably having more in common with the Shropshire lads who worked alongside Uncle Frank than sophisticated city dwellers from New York, Boston, Philadelphia and the East Coast, to say nothing of Californians and those from the Deep South. I also saw my first black men, who seemed not to mix with the white soldiers, although I knew from overheard

Doctors, nurses and others watch a patient being put aboard former Green Line 10T10 coach T454, now converted to an ambulance, during evacuation from Westminster Hospital on 1 September 1939. A masking cowl has already been fitted to the nearside headlamp of the coach, although the wingtip has not yet been painted white. The walls of the hospital are heavily sandbagged to protect them from blast damage.
London Transport Museum

conversations of my Shropshire relatives that black soldiers stationed there were certainly friendly with the local young women – whatever 'friendly' meant; clearly not quite the sort of relationships I shared with my friends on the farm. I was sitting on a Hants & Dorset bus one afternoon and two American soldiers on the seat in front were deep in conversation. They did nothing for the image of the loud, boasting GI, for I could hardly hear anything they said but I did catch a word I had not come across before — 'nostalgia'. I asked my mother what it meant and when she replied 'homesick', which was a feeling I knew only too well, having experienced it each time the war uprooted us, I began to see the young Americans in a different light.

The Clubmobile conversions and repaintings in grey were carried out by Samuel Elliott & Co of Caversham, following which they were sent on to R. G. Jones of Morden for fitting out with a record-player, radio, and amplifier. No doubt there were also plenty of Glenn Miller, Benny Goodman, Bob Crosby, Count Basie,

Duke Ellington and Dorsey Brothers records, for British big-band efforts were but a pale imitation of all-conquering American swing. Finally the vehicles went off to Dukes Yard, Grosvenor Square and were handed over to the US Red Cross, each one acquiring a crew of four young women and a driver.

Sixteen of the earlier Green Line T-class AEC Regal coaches of 1930/1, numbered in the range T207-306, were converted to London Transport staff ambulances. Retaining 11 seats, they were fitted with bunks and first-aid kits, painted olive green, renumbered in the service fleet and allocated to Central Area garages, Underground depots, works etc as follows:

T120 (456W)	Morden Underground depot, Merton bus garage
T209 (431W)	Neasden Underground depot, Cricklewood bus garage
T219 (428W)	Golders Green Underground depot, Hendon bus garage
T229 (430W)	Acton Works
T249 (438W)	Brixton tram depot, Streatham bus garage
T252 (424W)	Lillie Bridge Underground depot
T262 (435W)	Clapham tram depot
T264 (425W)	Wood Lane electrical engineers' depot, Hammersmith bus garage
T265 (433W)	Greenwich power station
T270 (429W)	Lots Road power station
T277 (434W)	New Cross tram depot, Nunhead bus garage
T290 (426W)	Parsons Green Works, Putney Bridge bus garage
T292 (432W)	Charlton Works
T297 (427W)	Ealing Common Underground depot, Southall bus garage
T301 (423W)	Fulwell trolleybus depot
T302 (437W)	Chiswick Works

Of these, T120 was from the earlier (1930-vintage), rear-entrance series and replaced T258 (436W). This latter had suffered bomb damage in October 1940 and was rebuilt in September 1941 as an open bolster lorry; as such it lasted until 1960, so London Transport certainly got its money's worth out of this vehicle, despite the efforts of Herr Hitler.

The eight Inter-Station Leyland Cubs were loaned to the official entertainment organisation, ENSA. The initials stood for 'Entertainments National Service Association' and *not*, as one wag suggested, for 'Every Night Something Atrocious', although this alternative provides a hint that, inevitably, the quality of the acts sent all over the country to military bases, factories engaged in war work etc varied considerably. At the top end the theatrical knights Laurence Olivier and Ralph Richardson performed Shakespeare — Olivier's film of *Henry V*, made during the war, with its stirring call to arms in the great speech before the Battle of Agincourt, was enormously popular — whilst variety stars such as Gracie Fields and George Formby were also recruited. But the customers might also be confronted by ventriloquists who were more wooden than their dummies and sopranos well into middle age warbling songs containing references to being sweet sixteen and never been kissed. Apparently the Cubs also received mixed notices, their large storage space being much appreciated, but not their shortage of breath in the more hilly regions of Northern England and Scotland.

Whilst on the subject of entertainment, which the Government recognised right from the outset of war as being of great importance in keeping up morale, on 2 October 1941 the LPTB Board of Directors were presented by the Executive Officer for Staff and Staff Welfare with a memorandum proposing 'to continue the arrangements instituted in July 1940 for the provision of music and lunch-time entertainment

One of the 10T10 Green Line coaches converted to a Clubmobile provides welcome hot drinks for what looks like a very chilly group of American servicemen in the winter of 1944. *Author's collection*

Above: Gracie Fields ('Our Gracie') singing to construction workers in 1941. Gracie Fields was just about the biggest British music-hall and film star of the 1930s and '40s. Recovering in Italy from cancer in 1940, she married Monty Banks, an Italian citizen who would have been interned had he stayed in the UK, so she and he went to America. An ill-informed press accused her of cowardice but she was soon back in the UK and touring the world wherever British and Empire troops were serving, boosting morale. Not surprisingly the public adored her; she never lost her Rochdale accent and was belatedly created a dame in 1979, the year she died. *Author's collection*

Left: A song much sung in the early years of the war and performed by Billy Cotton and his band. Billy Cotton, a somewhat larger-than-life character, whose catch phrase was 'Wakey, Wakey!' (roared out in a Cockney accent), was a fearless pilot of light aeroplanes and racing cars — he once drove *Bluebird*. He served in the Dardanelles in World War 1, was commissioned in the Royal Flying Corps in 1918 and was probably Britain's best-known band leader right through from the 1920s to his death in 1968. *Author's collection*

for staff employed in the Board's Works at Chiswick, Charlton and Acton'. The Board agreed to an expenditure of £2,000 for 1942.

Older readers may well remember *Workers' Playtime*, which began in 1941 and went out on the BBC's Home Service three times a week at lunchtime from a factory canteen 'somewhere in Britain'. Each show ended with the producer, Bill Gates' stirring exhortation 'Good Luck All Workers'. Rather like ENSA, it was something of a curate's egg in the quality of its performers, although it did provide a first exposure on the wireless for a number who would later become famous, amongst them Morecambe and Wise (called up to serve as miners — Bevin Boys, as they were called, after cabinet minister Ernest Bevin), Tony Hancock, Frankie Howerd, Julie Andrews — who began as a child star with her father and mother, Ted and Barbara — and Peter Sellers.

For a while, despite fuel reductions and withdrawal of many vehicles, production of buses and trolleybuses continued. The last standard STL arrived on 4 September, although the class would be added to on several subsequent occasions both during and after the war; the final member of the TF class also came that month, being immediately converted for war service, whilst a new class, the CR, which were 20-seat rear-engined Cubs and just about the last thing needed in wartime, began to arrive in

September. The first production RTs entered service from Chelverton Road (Putney) garage on 2 January 1940, the prototype having taken up ordinary passenger work from that garage on 9 August 1939.

The removal of the entire Green Line network caused much inconvenience and provoked considerable protest. This served its purpose, for the Government ordered the release of a number of coaches which had been converted to ambulances, and on 1 November 1939 the first of the restored services, those between Aldgate and Romford and Grays which had always been heavily used, reappeared. In all, 211 coaches were returned to London Transport, but many of the restored Green Line services were worked by STL double-deckers, so great was the demand.

With the continuation of the Phoney War and the approach of the 1940 Easter bank holiday and lengthening daylight hours, the Government, anxious to maintain morale, allowed London Transport to operate many extra Green Line coaches and buses out into the countryside, these being augmented by the usual holiday extensions to bus, tram and trolleybus routes. There were even leaflets produced advertising places of interest in Central London, the suburbs and the countryside which could be visited at weekends. In the middle of May 1940 summer schedules were introduced, at 75% of

Another source of scarce re-usable materials was old tram lines. Here the tracks are being dug up in Leyton in March 1940 to be 'sold for scrap for the manufacture of new armaments to help the National War Effort'. It was estimated the task would take six months and cost £73,000, but it was obviously considered worthwhile. In fact, many disused tram tracks were not recovered until decades afterwards; some were still visible, if one knew where to look, in the 21st century, and no doubt some remain to be uncovered by archæologists of the future. *London Transport Museum*

their 1938 level, but this coincided with the Nazi invasion of Holland, Belgium and France and the arrival of huge numbers of bewildered, non-English-speaking, and, inevitably, travel-weary and travel-stained refugees. Arriving by train from the South Coast they were met by fleets of buses and taken to Wembley Stadium and Alexandra Palace reception centres. Special measures were needed to clean the vehicles when this work was complete.

Next, with the prospect of imminent invasion, it was decided to evacuate as many of the population of South Coast towns as wished to move, and 530 double-deck buses and 20 single-deckers helped in the exodus. Despite this, once the Blitz began and our house eventually became badly knocked about, although just about still habitable, we headed in the opposite direction, my mother, grandmother and myself renting a bungalow near Bognor whilst Dad came down, when he could, to visit us at weekends. Thus I swapped journeys on red AECs for jaunts on green Southdown Leyland Titans and became entranced by the deep roar of their engines. I have only to hear a preserved Titan or Tiger from that era to be instantly transported back to those days beside the sea. Living at the seaside, now that really was something, a pleasurable change in circumstances which I had never envisaged as a possibility. I discovered an abandoned bicycle in the garage and rode it about the quiet roads leading to the beach, and made friends with Peter, whom I deeply envied, for he was old enough to go to school. I kept the bicycle for many years until I had long outgrown it, and if Peter should happen to read this I can confirm that my schooldays, spent at a variety of establishments on account of the war, were generally all he had promised.

I missed the London trams and although I developed a lifelong affection for Southdown buses not all my journeys passed without incident. The furnishings of a Short Bros-bodied Titan, although perfectly acceptable, were rather different from those of a Chiswick-inspired interior and on one journey, sitting beside my father upstairs near the back I was intrigued by a small, circular fitting which gave way when I pushed it. The bus was fairly empty, but the conductor came up several times — not, seemingly, to collect fares but to stare hard at the few passengers. My father, reading his paper, had not noticed. Finally the conductor called out in a loud voice, 'Who keeps pushing that damned bell?' Dad put his paper down, looked at me, then at the bell push conveniently placed beside me, and truth dawned on all three of us. Obviously London buses had bell pushes but

presumably I had never come across one so handily placed.

On another occasion we went out for the day to Arundel and a trip on the river, not by Southdown but in an ancient single-decker, belonging to an outfit known as Silver Queen, on which all of us, the driver included, sat cosily together and I could watch the driver operating the gear lever, brakes and steering wheel, but not the air-conditioning, a feature which was decades into the future. This was rather a pity, as the atmosphere on the way back, my stomach already a little queasy from the rippling waters of the River Arun, grew ever more stuffy and oppressive until Dad had to ask the driver to stop so I could be sick on the grass verge. Still very much the worse for wear, I had to be carried home, to my great mortification, for Peter was watching for our return.

Dad and I took a trip to Horsham, not I think to allay any nostalgic leanings I might have evinced for the London Country shade of green, for even a four-year-old could see that the Southdown livery of two-tone green and generous helpings of cream was quite the finest he was ever likely to encounter, but to establish my maturity by staying at a hotel for the night without my mother — presumably she had to remain behind to mind Granny. This was accomplished, I being much impressed by the thick, linen napkins and the big, shiny cutlery provided by the hotel. Part of the journey there was in a vehicle furnished in a manner quite outside my previous experience, a single-decker with seats arranged around the perimeter which was all right if one found the passengers opposite particularly attractive or peculiar, but not so good if one preferred looking out of the window. This would have been one of the Southdown '1400' series of TS7 and TS8 Leyland Tigers which were adapted during the war to standee layout to accommodate extra standing passengers. To this day, being very much a double-deck sort of person, I still find single-deckers slightly exotic.

Like just about every other bus operator, London Transport adapted a number of its single-deckers to 'standee' layout; double-deckers were unsuited to such modifications. I have a friend, Betty Ackerman, who in her wartime memoirs describes riding to school in just such a single-decker. 'It was laid out in the strangest way — seats across the back as usual but then a long seat down each side to make the maximum space for people to stand in the centre. These seats were mainly for ladies with very small children, large ladies with large wicker baskets, pregnant ladies, elderly people, the blind and the

A 1939-vintage Southdown Harrington-bodied TS8 Leyland Tiger of the type that was altered to 'standee' layout to increase capacity. *Author*

lame. We as school children were the very last on the list so even though we might be first in the queue we went immediately to the far end of the bus and stood on the two steps leading to the emergency exit. The satchels on our backs were knobbly with two straps and buckles, so we took them off and laid them at our feet. The bus filled up behind us, members of the forces in full pack, people with shopping and then the conductor would shout "Move up, there are three more to get on," and we would shuffle up as close as we could because we knew what it was to be left behind. We were standing pretty much on the steps and when we reached our stop we opened the emergency door and jumped down into the road. It sounds very dangerous but petrol was so severely rationed that there was hardly any traffic. Someone closed the door behind us and no doubt took our places. At the beginning of the war when everything had to be blacked out, the buses had their windows painted dark blue with just a narrow strip left that we could look through. We learned to know where we were by the twists and turns in the road.'

Betty had a cousin, John, who had been living with his parents in Malta; his father was in the

REME. She writes that 'more bombs fell on Malta in six months than fell on London in the whole of the war. People had to take to the caves … and Uncle told me that the children were lined up once a month and given ONE boiled sweet as a treat. The mothers and children were eventually evacuated via Egypt and right around Africa. Cousin John arrived with a tennis ball which he bounced ceaselessly and a tin of Golden Syrup which was his alone as he needed building up. He was as white as a sheet and so thin, every time a door slammed or there was a sudden sharp sound he jumped out of his skin.'

We were living a short distance from Tangmere, one of the most famous Battle of Britain aerodromes and today a museum and memorial to that period. Dad and I would often walk up a country lane to where a four-wheel trap had been left by a gateway, its motive power long departed, and upon which we and our dog, Trix, would sit and watch Hurricanes and Spitfires taking off and landing. Although I

The author, with his father and their dog Trix, sitting in a farmer's trap near RAF Tangmere, September 1940. *Author's collection*

Battle of Britain aircrew at RAF Tangmere, September 1940. *Author's collection*

didn't know it at the time, Douglas Bader was there, in charge of 219 Squadron, which exchanged its Hurricanes for Spitfires in January 1941. Many years later I photographed Spitfires and Hurricanes at RAF Kenley when the film of Bader's extraordinary career, *Reach for the Sky*, starring Kenneth More as Bader, was being filmed there. Kenley was served by Country Area route 453. Bader lost his legs in a crash in 1931 and was not expected to live, but he not only survived but managed to persuade the RAF to let him rejoin as a pilot in 1939. He was eventually shot down and captured, but the Germans allowed the RAF to parachute replacement artificial legs for him and he was released in time to lead the victory flypast over Buckingham Palace in the summer of 1945.

Reach for the Sky came out in 1956 and became the most popular British film of the year.

The last RAF squadron left Tangmere in October 1970, and part of the site is now occupied by Tangmere Military Aviation Museum, which I visited while researching this book, on a warm summer morning — just the sort of weather in which the Battle of Britain was fought. Two replica Spitfires and a replica Hurricane are displayed there, along with many actual artefacts from 1940/1. Perhaps the most poignant is a section of a Spitfire, the cockpit surprisingly intact, shot down during the Battle of Britain. It was only discovered, buried deep in the ground, more than 40 years later, excavated, and brought to Tangmere. Above, light aircraft from nearby Goodwood appeared

London Transport staff trimming electrical wires for use in aircraft in 1942. These were all volunteers, working in their spare time, and in this manner they contributed over £200,000 worth of free labour. *London Transport Museum*

in the sky from time to time, their piston engines making a noise not so unlike that made by the Merlin engines of Spitfires and Hurricanes; the following day the Red Arrows hurtled past on their way from a D-Day commemoration display.

Arguably the most famous RAF Fighter Command base of all was Biggin Hill, and London Transport Country Area route 410 from Bromley to Reigate passed right through it. From 26 May 1940 the service was curatailed, buses turning round either side of the aerodrome. Later a diversion, using 20-seat Leyland Cub single-deckers, came into operation, but it wasn't until January 1942 that Godstone garage's lowbridge STLs resumed their original route, and even then passengers could not get out whilst the bus was traversing the airfield, and an armed sentry climbed aboard, presumably without having to pay, to ensure no-one attempted to.

Back in London, Chiswick Works had become involved in the Battle of Britain, overhauling the Rolls-Royce Merlin engines used in Spitfires. Before the war London Transport had been planning what became known in 1941 as the London Aircraft Production Group. This was done in conjunction with Handley Page, which was based at Radlett in Hertfordshire. Chiswick and Aldenham works, the latter originally intended as a depot for the Northern Line, took on production of the Handley Page Halifax bomber, turning out 710 of these by 1945. In all 6,176 were built, one an hour when production was at its peak.

Never as famous as the Lancaster, the Halifax was nevertheless a vital component of Bomber Command's strike force. After the war Halifaxes assumed all sorts of roles, some being converted to makeshift airliners, others taking part in the Berlin Airlift, but none survived for very long, all being scrapped before any serious thoughts were given to preservation. However, although no Halifax will ever fly again, two can be seen, complete, in museums. One, recovered from a Norwegian lake, is in Canada; the other, reconstructed from various parts, is at the Yorkshire Air Museum. A third, also removed from Norwegian waters, is on display at the RAF Museum, Hendon, in the condition in which it was recovered.

A Halifax bomber (one of 710 which London Transport helped build), Central Area bus STL1235 with partly boarded-up windows and a group of workers, probably at Leavesden, where the completed aircraft were tested. *London Transport Museum*

4

The fleet 1939-41

Production of motor buses and trolleybuses was, initially, unaffected by the outbreak of war. Thirty-nine 'L3' and 'N1' trolleys which had just been delivered ready for a tram conversion scheme were immediately licensed on 1 September to help with evacuations, whilst on 10 September East London tram route 77 became trolleybus route 677 and more new trolleybuses took up work, from Hackney depot. The all-Leyland 'K' types at Hackney depot had wartime adaptations, such as restricted lighting and white edging to the front mudguards and at the rear, but in all essentials were to full prewar specification. This was far from the end of 'prewar'-type trolleybuses, for the fleet would continue to expand, and the tram fleet contract, into 1941, whilst the actual replacement of trams by trolleybuses, which had begun far away in the west

Workmen removing track in Hackney depot in March 1939 momentarily cease their labours for a photograph to be taken. Behind the 'E1' trams is a 'K'-type trolleybus ready to replace the trams. *London Transport Museum*

'E1' tram No 1050 approaching the King's Road, Chelsea, terminus of route 32 in the summer of 1939. This was one of the last cars to be fitted with a windscreen, this being done in June 1941. *Author's collection*

in the Kingston area in 1931, would go on in the east, just in time to meet the full force of the Nazi onslaught on the East End and the London Docks.

On 5 November 1939 the trams working routes 61 and 63 from Bow depot were replaced by a fleet of handsome BRCW- and Park Royal-bodied 'N1' and 'N2' AEC trolleybuses for routes 661 and 663. Five days later a gap in the trolleybus empire was filled when the Highgate Hill tram route 11, operated by the 'HR2' class (the initials standing for 'Hilly Route'), became trolleybus route 611. Already delivered 'J3s' and 'L1s' fitted with special coasting brakes were allocated to the 611. The 'HR2s' were far too modern to be scrapped and moved south to the Dog Kennel Hill routes at Dulwich. Three, however, were sold to Leeds. Finally, on 9 June 1940, the 65 and 67 routes worked by Poplar depot gave way to the 565, the 665 and the 567. Chassisless AEC 'L3s' with MCW bodies filled Poplar depot. Any doubts there might have been as to the viability of this method of construction proved groundless, 'L3s' lasting until the very last day of trolleybus operation in London. One of Poplar's 'L3s', No 1521, is preserved at the East Anglia Transport Museum at Carlton Colville, near Lowestoft.

Although this was the last instance of trams' being replaced by trolleybuses, 50 more Leyland trolleys were on order, these being needed in case of service increases or, more likely, to replace those destroyed or damaged by enemy action. They began to arrive in September 1940, although delivery was not completed until a year later. The first 25 were all-Leyland 'K3s', almost identical to the 'K1s' and 'K2s' and therefore rather old-fashioned looking, with no radiused windows, but the remainder, the

Metro-Cammell-bodied 'P1s', were right up to date in appearance, very like the 'L3s' but somewhat loftier, having separate chassis. Despite arriving so late — the final 'P1', No 1721, not beginning work until 1 October 1941, more than two years after war had been declared — they were fully up to peacetime standards, other than being panelled in steel rather than aluminium, which made them a little heavier.

Withdrawal of trams — although not necessarily scrapping — continued until May 1940. Many redundant 'E1s' were stored in Hampstead depot and were brought out later to replace cars damaged or destroyed. Many of the less severely damaged cars took their places in store in case they might eventually be needed and thus repaired. Purley depot was also used and many redundant 'E1s', without windscreens, sat there, gathering dust, well beyond the end of the war. Fitting of windscreens had begun in the mid-1930s but was not completed until October 1941, when any East Ham 'E1s' still without them were dealt with.

How tram drivers were able to take out cars without windscreens in January 1940 is beyond comprehension, for it was the coldest month since February 1895. Temperatures sank below –20°C, people skated on six-inch-thick ice on the Serpentine, the Thames froze for eight miles between Teddington and Sunbury, and ice and snowstorms battered London and the South East, causing widespread disruption to public transport. There has never been anything like the ice storm of 27 January. Drivers of cars found themselves trapped, the door locks frozen, umbrellas put up in the freezing rain turned into solid ice, birds fell from the air, their wings iced in mid-flight, London Transport garages ran out of anti-

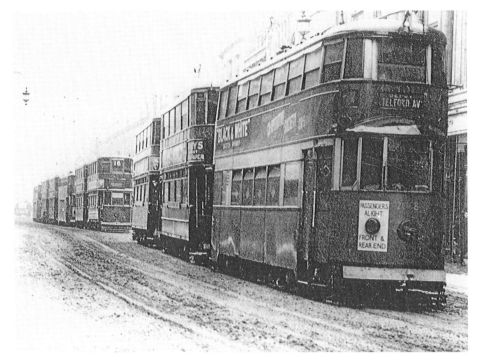

A line of trams, headed by a 'Feltham', during the freezing conditions of January 1940. *Author's collection*

freeze, and out in the Country Area the roads in the hilly areas of the North Downs and the Chilterns in particular became ice rinks and impassable. The scale of the ice storm was kept from the general public lest the enemy should take advantage of the almost complete cessation of movement.

A move to augment the fleet (which has never been fully explained) is recorded in a memorandum submitted to the LPTB directors on 7 November 1940 following an appeal made the previous month. 'The General Manager (Operation) … reporting upon the traffic situation, and the steps which have been taken to provide alternative transport by bus to replace railway, tramway and trolleybus services damaged by enemy action. To overcome the difficulty of a shortage of buses, the Ministry of Transport and the Regional Commissioners throughout the country have so far secured the loan of about 500 buses for use in London upon terms to be arranged.' Many have since wondered just why such a large number was needed,

Aldgate bus station in 1940, with two roofbox STLs. Nearer the camera is one of the final batch, STL2600, delivered in 1939 and working Green Line service Z1 to Grays, alongside the slightly older STL2321 of Hackney garage. Both buses still retain full destination displays. *London Transport Museum*

Two STLs from Streatham garage (AK) at the Clapham Common terminus of route 118, c1941. Both have advertisements for war savings and white-painted mudguards and platform edges. STL1655 still has a prewar-style set of blinds; STL1407, at the rear, has a restricted display and also has at least one window with netting over it and a diamond cut out so passengers can see out. *Author's collection*

for although there had, indeed, been much damage to London's own buses, there had also been a huge reduction in the number of buses required daily. Many of those damaged had been rapidly patched up and put back to work, quite often with windows boarded over, and whilst it is true that there was disruption to tram, trolleybus and Underground services these were usually restored pretty quickly; moreover, new trolleybuses were still being delivered, and the trams replaced were not being scrapped but kept in reserve. Did the Board and the authorities anticipate that the situation, dire though it was, could only get worse, and that although London Transport staff were going to extraordinary lengths, well beyond the call of duty, to restore and keep services running, they would eventually be overwhelmed? If so they were

unnecessarily pessimistic, for although terrible havoc would continue to be wrought upon London well into 1941 — in fact until the German invasion of Russia in June that year drew most of the Luftwaffe efforts to the Eastern front — some of the provincial buses returned within days, scheduled operation of them came to an end in the late summer of 1941, and by early 1942 London, as we shall discover in a later chapter, was lending buses to the provinces.

5

Underground preparations

On 1 September 1939 the Railway Executive Committee began work, overseeing the London Underground and the main-line railways and ensuring that their principal efforts were directed to sustaining and winning the war. Seventy-two Underground stations received evacuees and took them to outlying stations for their onward journeys. One of the greatest concerns in relation to the Underground was what would happen if enemy bombs breached tunnels under the Thames. Water could have flooded deep into the system causing almost unimaginable chaos. London Transport had been considering the problem long before September 1939. Floodgates were clearly the answer, but in the restricted tunnels much ingenuity had to be employed in order to install the 25 which were ultimately placed in position. The autumn of 1938 when Britain so nearly went to war — there is a picture in our family album entitled 'Munich Crisis 1938' of my father and I sitting atop the just completed Anderson shelter — provided a dummy run when blocks of concrete were inserted in the Northern and Bakerloo Line tunnels between Charing Cross and Waterloo and left for some 10 days whilst trains reversed either side of them. The blocks were put in place in 24 hours; it took four days to remove them and get the trains running again.

Although it was the Tube lines which crossed under the Thames in Central London, the District and Inner Circle Lines running along the Embankment were equally vulnerable, as was the East London line using Brunel's original Thames tunnel. Floodgates, 13in thick and weighing around 10 tons each, were installed at Waterloo on the Bakerloo and Northern Lines and on the other side of the river at the Strand and Charing Cross. They could be closed in 30 seconds, by hand if necessary should the two electrical supplies fail. These gates were capable of resisting a force of 800 tons, several times greater than any water pressure they might

have had to confront. Six rather smaller gates, weighing four and a half tons each, were installed in the passages connecting the District and Northern Lines at Charing Cross. A back-up system, should these precautions fail, was put in place at 10 locations.

Various devices and means of communication were put in place to cover the eventualities of, for example, a train being in a tunnel when an alert sounded or phone lines being put out of commission. Despite tremendous damage being inflicted on the Underground, it does not seem that flooding on a totally disastrous scale ever did take place; certainly no bomb penetrated the bed of the Thames. A bomb beside Tooting Broadway station on 7 October 1940 did, however, penetrate water mains, resulting in many deaths. As in many other locations, the floodgates are still there.

Despite the certainty that there would be war some newspapers insisted, right through the summer of 1939, that peace would prevail. As late as 1 September the *Kentish Independent* reported that the prospective National Conservative candidate for Dartford, one David Behar, had told a meeting of the Belvedere North Conservative Club that, having lived in Germany for some years, '... I have made a close study of the economic situation in Germany' and that 'I do not think we are to be confronted by a war'. In the same edition the paper reported that 'the Blackheath branch of the Peace Pledge Union ... held a meeting in support of peace'. Unfortunately they had failed to persuade Herr Hitler to join, and the paper went on to record that not only was 'far more attention given to the public activities nearby of the anti-aircraft detachments and troop movements', but that more realistic counsels had prevailed upon the local authorities to have 'the trenches at Blackheath ... reopened and kept under the supervision of L.C.C. park-keepers'. As the official London Transport publication of 1947 –

London Transport Carried On, by Charles Graves — records, 489 buses were employed on two days in the last week of August 1939 in moving three divisions of anti-aircraft personnel to their war stations in various parts of the Home Counties. The headquarters of Anti-Aircraft Control was set up in a disused Underground station.

The next paragraph of the *Kentish Independent* of 1 September 1939 is headed 'Black-Out Lights' and reads thus: 'On Wednesday morning buses on local routes appeared with a white painted line around the platform and on the stairs leading to the upper deck. All buses, trams and trolleybuses have now been equipped with "black-out lights" inside and out.'

Trains and stations were almost completely blacked-out, and whilst far fewer people travelled on the Underground after dark it was realised that conditions were dangerous, and safety reading lamps were developed and installed. As men went off to war so women took up a variety of jobs on the Underground, as well as on buses, trams and trolleybuses.

Whilst much of the intended new works on the Underground came to a halt on the outbreak of war, notably those planned in conjunction with the GWR and the LNER, and various cutbacks in order to save power were instituted — escalators, for example, often only operated during the rush hours — not all planned improvements were put on hold. Amongst the services which came to an end was the GWR one to Liverpool Street and Aldgate. The Metropolitan Line electric locomotives which used to take over from GWR steam at Bishop's Road station, Paddington, were eventually scrapped but the close-coupled, six-coach rakes of specially built suburban GWR carriages continued in use on suburban services out of Paddington, four of them serving on miners' trains in South Wales as late as 1964, thus lasting into the preservation era, so that Brake Third No 3755 has been restored by the Great Western Society at Didcot

Passengers alight from a District Line train of brand-new 'Metadyne' stock in the summer of 1939. *London Transport Museum*

to the ornate livery which it carried when it first entered service and regularly ran on the Inner Circle. In the opposite direction the through trains which ran by way of the former London, Tilbury & Southend line from the Thames Estuary resort to Ealing Broadway ceased. Neither service was ever revived, although Cross Rail will replicate much of both.

The businessmen's Pullmans which the Metropolitan Line ran out to the Chilterns were withdrawn, as were through peak-hour Hammersmith & City trains between New Cross and New Cross Gate and Hammersmith. The depot at Aldenham, intended to service Northern Line trains on the proposed extension from Edgware to Elstree and Bushey Heath, was well on the way to completion, but the extension would never be built and Aldenham would after the war become London Transport's principal bus-overhaul works.

The one LNER service which did pass into Underground control during the war was that to High Barnet, Northern Line trains replacing LNER steam on 14 April 1940. Just as new trolleybuses and RT motor buses continued to arrive well into 1941, so delivery of 1938 Tube stock and 'P' and 'Q' surface stock went ahead for some time, if at an ever decreasing rate until it ceased altogether, although the postwar 'R' stock, the first of which appeared in 1949, looked almost identical to 'P' and 'Q' cars.

A unique new wartime vintage Underground vehicle was No L10, which was employed as the Acton Works shunter. *Modern Transport* on 10 May 1941 described it in some detail with the sub-heading 'Built Largely from Discarded Material'. Ever since the outbreak of war the general public had been urged to 'make do and mend' and throw nothing away if it could be avoided, so a diesel-line electric locomotive (what the Southern Region would later call an electro-diesel) which followed these precepts, its only new parts being its diesel engine, the electric generator and some switchgear, the rest being parts from two old Central Line motor cars, was clearly to be welcomed. It could act as a straight electric locomotive, taking current from the third rail, or as a diesel-electric, the current being provided by its own generator set. Capable of hauling 600 tons on the level, it pointed the way to the future.

6

War comes to London

The Blitz proper began on 7 September 1940, a day of clear skies and brilliant sunshine. The sirens, that stomach-churning rising and falling moan, sounded at teatime, and the bombs began to fall on the Docks and the surrounding areas. After an hour and a quarter of hell there was a two-hour pause but then, in the darkness, even worse followed with wave after wave of bombers breaking through the defences and devastating the East End and the City of London. Until then the Battle of Britain had been fought largely over the fields, villages and towns of Kent, Surrey and Sussex and the English Channel as the Luftwaffe attempted to wipe out the RAF and its airfields and installations preparatory to Hitler launching the seaborne invasion of Britain. But now, apparently provoked by an RAF raid on Berlin, provoked in turn by an isolated raid on Central London, Hitler set out to destroy the capital and to bludgeon its population into submission. The promised terror from the sky, expected ever since September 1939, had arrived.

Much as Londoners and London suffered, the switch of tactics by the Luftwaffe almost certainly lost the war for Germany. In the two weeks immediately before 7 September the RAF had 295 Hurricanes and Spitfires destroyed and 231 pilots killed or wounded. If RAF losses had continued at that rate it could not have sustained its efforts for very much longer. But by ending its raids on Fighter Command's bases and concentrating its bomber force on London the Luftwaffe handed the initiative to the RAF. The most decisive day was 15 September when the RAF claimed to have shot down 185 enemy aircraft, losing only 25 itself. Years later, after the war, the Luftwaffe losses were scaled down to around 60. But whatever the precise figure the destruction of so many aircraft did wonders not just for Fighter Command's morale but for the nation's. On 17 September, by which time Hitler had lost a quarter of his bomber force, he announced the postponement of the invasion of Great Britain.

A week before the raids of 7 September the *Croydon Advertiser* had reported an almost light-hearted, *blasé* attitude to 'raids that lasted for six and seven hours'. The report began by describing 'The first long night raid of the war in the London area', but this gave absolutely no clue to the horrors which would shortly befall the capital. 'From 9.30pm until well into Tuesday morning people came out of their shelters to stretch their legs, or those whose curiosity kept them out of shelter, saw a wonderful display of searchlight beams all round ... Many people were caught on buses and trams a long way from home. Some stayed with friends, others in public shelters ... The piercing rays — of the searchlights — diligently searched every inch of cloud space, and whenever a Nazi essayed to come down low he was quickly picked up and there would follow reports of the anti-aircraft guns with their red stars bursting all around the aircraft. Mostly, however, the aircraft preferred to keep at a great height and it appeared they were more intent on making a nuisance of themselves ... little damage was done and nothing was dropped in the Croydon area ... When the all-clear sounded at about 4am, there was a long stream of buses passing through the district with weary-eyed but still cheerful passengers.' It is interesting that whilst this first report refers to the 'Croydon area' subsequent accounts of where bombs were dropped and casualties sustained use terms such as 'a southern district near London'.

Having conquered France, the Luftwaffe was able to build airfields close to the French coast and send fighters to escort its bombers across the Channel. More than 1,000 German aircraft took part in the raid of 7 September, the first of 57 consecutive nights of bombing on London. On that first night 448 people were killed. Huge disruption was caused to London Transport bus, tram, trolleybus and Underground services although, rather remarkably, relatively little actual damage to vehicles or property. To quote Ken Glazier, in *London Buses and the Second*

World War (Capital Transport, 1986), 'The very act of taking a vehicle out onto the streets became one of heroism in itself.'

The following are quotes from the *Battle of Britain Campaign Diary* of the RAF — 'Soon after 17.00 hours … the enemy launched a very big attack and the principal objectives seem to have been industrial and dock property on both sides of the Thames; bombs were dropped at Woolwich, Purfleet and the Dockland area of London … there has been considerable interference with rail and road communications in the area. At Purfleet, serious fires occurred at the Anglo-American Oil Works and other industrial buildings were hit and fires broke out. In Dockland, principally in the East India, West India, Surrey Commercial and Millwall Dock very serious fires broke out, due to the large number of bombs … Possibly the most serious effect has been in Silvertown which has been described as a "raging inferno" and complete evacuation became necessary. Over 600 fire appliances were in use during the night.'

Ken Glazier writes of those East Enders fleeing westwards, 'The appearance of these people was pitiable: they were dirty and dusty, had torn clothing and many were in a state of shock. To the luckier residents of the West End and inner West London, the sight of the victims using public transport sometimes proved too much; unbelievably many complaints were made.' He adds that this was not the attitude of the crews, who may well have come from the devastated areas themselves and feared for their families but carried on working. Amongst all the stories of courage and stoicism there are many of fear, panic and despair, and why not? We cannot all be heroes and if we have an imagination then war is just about the most appalling experience it is possible to undergo. For some it was too much to bear. The *Kentish Independent* of 15 September 1939 reported the inquest on an Erith mother who had cut the throat of her four-year-old son and then her own. Her husband, an ARP worker, said that his wife 'was terribly upset by the war, that she had said that "Mr Chamberlain and Hitler were fast friends who had worked the war to create a panic" '. She had not slept for a fortnight.

The *Ilford Recorder* of 19 September 1940 reported the experiences of one of its correspondents. He had

One of the saddest pictures of the Blitz the author has ever come across. A policeman hands a cup of tea to an elderly East Ender who has returned home from work to find his house destroyed and his wife dead. *Author's collection*

got a lift in an ambulance driven by a young woman, uncertain of her route, and he had guided her. 'Bombs were dropping around us as we neared our destination and fires were starting.' They park and the correspondent 'nosed around, questioned residents, and dodged bombs. One man, at his door, was in the last war. He scorned dugouts. A man of 20, leading a greyhound, called from the other side of the road, "Hi guv'nor! Help me, please!"

"What is it?" I asked.

"Show me home, guv'nor. I only live up there but lead me to it. I was all alone. I feel terrible."

I told him that was natural and told him not to worry.

"They seemed as if they were making for me, guv'nor."

"Yes, it always seems like that, but they aren't."

"See what it was, guv'nor, they were shutting me in."

"Yes, but it's alright now."

"I'm alright now, guv'nor, but just for a bit I couldn't seem to think. I can get home now."'

In the same issue a Mr S. Lewis, who lived with his family in a flat in Ilford and had no shelter, described what happened as they made for the railway station as the raid began.

'A bomb dropped on the platform opposite. I shouted to the wife to drop and she and the children did so. I flopped on top of them. We shall never have a narrower escape than that. Our mouths were full of dust and we were covered with debris.' A train was approaching the station. 'Men on the platform shouted to the driver, and he managed to stop his train — a through passenger — as he reached the damaged part of the line. Part of the train was derailed but there were no casualties.'

The following are the words of George Turnbull, a member of the Home Guard in Limehouse: "My God, what on earth is happening? This is it … we're finished. But of course this was really only the beginning. Explosions were everywhere, there just was not a break, bang after bang after bang. The clang of bells from fire service vehicles and ambulances was drowned out by those bombs. You would hear a whistle as a stick of bombs came down, then a loud explosion as they hit factories and houses and the ground shook. Then as soon as that explosion happened another whistle and another explosion. God, this seemed to go on for hours."

Altogether 181 members of the London Transport staff would be killed whilst on duty during the air attacks on London and 1,867 were injured, whilst a further 245 died whilst off duty, with 1,006 injured.

Nineteen Underground carriages were destroyed, together with 16 trolleybuses, 69 trams and around 80 buses, while hundreds of others were damaged to a greater or lesser extent. Most of these losses were suffered in the bombing of depots at night. Staff in the depots were killed and injured, but at least no passengers died. However, in other incidents they certainly did. Many passengers on their way to work were killed and many more injured when two 'E1s' were destroyed by a direct hit from a bomb which penetrated the railway bridge in the Blackfriars Road in the morning peak on 25 October 1940, and were destroyed, with a third 'E1' and an 'E3' badly damaged. On the most horrendous night of all, 29/30 December 1940 (of which more in Chapter 8), a tram received a direct hit on the Embankment, killing the conductor and four passengers, and three trams were burned out at Camberwell, although fortunately the only casualty was an injured conductor. Southwark and Blackfriars Bridges were impassable and several tramway substations were damaged. There were thousands of incidents involving less than terminal damage to LT vehicles, which in almost all cases were repaired and put back into service.

The first severe, and much the greatest, loss to the tram fleet took place on the night of 8 September 1940 when Camberwell depot was hit and 29 cars

Two young East End women, having spent the night in an Underground station, are seen next morning salvaging what they can from their bombed home, September 1940. *Author's collection*

Above: Office workers picking their way through the rubble after a night of bombing in the City of London, September 1940. Author's collection

Left: East Enders the morning after a raid in September 1940. Author's collection

Opposite top: Workmen stand amongst the tangled wreckage at Camberwell tram depot on 11 September 1940. Twenty-nine trams, including both members of the 'HR1' class, were destroyed and many others damaged. London Transport Museum

Opposite bottom: Workers begin clearing what remains of the six destroyed tramcars and the many damaged ones at Abbey Wood depot on the morning of 8 November 1940. *London Transport Museum*

were destroyed. Eleven cars were destroyed when Clapham depot was hit on 15 September 1940, two more when it was again bombed on 16 April 1941. Abbey Wood depot was hit on 7 November 1940, and six cars were destroyed. Three were destroyed when New Cross depot was hit on 21 December 1940, but although most of the other depots received bomb damage, some on more than one occasion (Holloway, for example, was hit three times) no other tram was rendered a write-off.

The first collective destruction of the bus fleet took place on 22 October 1940 when a direct hit on the Bull Yard at Peckham wiped out 53 vehicles in store there. Amongst these were all but one of the 12 handsome TF-class touring coaches, scarcely a year old, 13 other single-deckers — one T, one CR and 11 LTs — and 29 ST double-deckers, 20 of them elderly Tillings with open staircases, time-expired but still much needed for the duration.

Initially, as soon as the air raid sirens sounded buses, trams and trolleybuses stopped and passengers and crews made for the nearest shelters, but after a while, as air raids became the norm (however hellish that norm), the crews kept their vehicles on the move unless they felt that the intensity of the guns and the proximity of bombs were such that they had to stop.

ARP wardens rescue a young woman from the basement of her bombed East End house, October 1940. *Author's collection*

The following quote from a driver was typical of the attitude of many: 'I never believed in parking up a bus, as I considered it was in Mr Hitler's favour to do so. In driving a bus for the public, I always considered I had a weapon of war in my hand, and it was up to me to use it to advantage against the enemy.' Another driver said, 'Strangely enough, it seemed that people felt safe when travelling on a bus, and had every confidence in the driver, and it helped us considerably to keep going when we continually got a "Good-night, driver, and thank you".'

In a sense, although a bus was certainly a large, formidable-looking object, the confidence in its impregnability was illusory. London buses were not built to last more than 10 years, and only then after several complete overhauls. Because of war shortages many had to last much longer, and the sag and general deterioration in their bodies of thin steel and glass fixed to wood framing became ever more evident. Trams were rather more substantial but far from invulnerable. Of course, in a collision between a tram and another vehicle the tram was likely to come off best. I was once sitting upstairs at the front of an 'E1' passing Streatham Common when I heard a tremendous crash at the rear. A motor cycle combination had tried to pass between the tram and a parked car and had not made it. My mother, who refused to let me leave my seat, assured me that the motor cyclist had suffered only a few cuts and bruises and 'would be all right' but I had — and have — my doubts that he escaped so relatively lightly. Being in a tram, bus or trolleybus in an air raid was probably preferable to being in the street but, rather like sitting under the stairs at home during an air raid, a near miss, let alone a direct hit, might well blow everything to pieces leaving, in the case of the vehicle, only its chassis and wheels still recognisable. But as one tram driver put it, '… there is an advantage in driving a tram rather than a bus. You can't hear a bomb coming or an aeroplane overhead. You don't know anything about what's happening.'

One of the greatest causes of injuries during air raids was flying glass fragments. To militate against this anti-blast netting was stuck on to windows by a coat of thick varnish, but this did not begin until September 1940. The netting rendered the windows opaque and inevitably passengers, frustrated at not seeing where they were, attempted to pick at this covering. After various experiments a small diamond area was left clear and this worked pretty well, although it was still rather frustrating, and I can recall seeing windows where some of the covering had been

A distinctly careworn STL1297 at the West Croydon terminus of route 75. Most of the windows are covered with netting with a diamond peephole and, by the looks of the open windows, including the windscreen, the weather must have been warm. *W. J. Haynes*

scraped away. But in general the glue was pretty tough and proved devilishly difficult to remove after the war.

We lived in Broughton Road, Thornton Heath, and trams on the 16, 18 and 42 routes passed 100 yards or so away along the London Road. The next two roads were Dunheved Road North and Dunheved Road South, the latter where my friend Keith, whose father was Croydon's deputy head librarian, lived. All this ceased on the night of 2/3 October 1940 when a bomb fell on London Road, between the two Dunheveds. Adjacent houses suffered from blast damage but the worst sufferers were the main road and the tram tracks which were destroyed, a huge crater being left in the road. Fortunately for Keith, the two Dunheved Roads were linked at the opposite end to the London Road and he was thus able to walk to school next morning. It being night time, all the trams serving these routes were in their depots at the Pond or Telford Avenue, so, although next morning trams could run from Thornton Heath Pond on the 42 to Thornton Heath High Street or on the 16 and 18 to London, Tilling ST buses had to be substituted for the trams south of the bomb crater, until four of the windscreen-less 'E1s' stored at Purley depot could be made serviceable and put to work on a shuttle service. This lasted until 15 October when a temporary track was laid across the hole.

One of the problems with a bomb crater was that this might contain an unexploded bomb and nothing could be done until it had been rendered harmless. Each day of the Blitz saw an average of 84 unexploded bombs. The courage of the bomb disposal crews who carried out such a hazardous task defies description. But then there were so many heroes during the Blitz, not least the London Transport employees who performed miracles either in keeping services going or getting them running again after an air raid.

But not everyone was a hero. This is the Yardmaster at Elephant & Castle, describing the incidents of a particularly terrible night, that of 10 May 1941. Every building in the vicinity was in flames and 'it seemed highly probable that they would envelop the station'. He collected five members of staff and 'appealed for volunteers among the male shelterers. To [my] astonishment, only one warden and an old man of 60 agreed to help …

Home Guards were about in the streets on account of some looting that was started by some of the rough element in the neighbourhood.'

Bill Maile was a driver at Croydon garage. This remarkable man, who celebrated his 100th birthday in September 2004, recalled the night of 11 May 1941. 'We were the last bus back. The buses were being re-fuelled and parked in the garage, and I said to the general hand on duty, "It seems a shame, all those buses should be left there. It only wants one on here and it would be a complete loss." That same night about eight bombs dropped in the locality. It was the only night I could not rest; I ate my supper standing I was so worried. So much did I have a kind of premonition, that I took off the suit I was wearing, it being new, and dressed in an old suit. I put the new one down the shelter for safety.

'I said to my wife: "Something has happened at the garage, I must go round there." I live about four or five minutes' walk away from the garage, and it was then about five to three in the morning. Four bombs had then fallen — two of them on our garage — it was a raging furnace. I looked at the buses and the garage, and grabbed all the time cards from the lockers and put them in my pocket as I thought a roll-call would be needed, and then I thought to myself: "The best thing to do is to save some buses." There was no one else about at the time.

'I ran one bus out and put it in the road. The next one I found locked and had to leave it.' He got all the front line safely out but the next were all on fire, although the fire brigade has now arrived and is playing water on them. He then got around to the back of the garage and got more out, plus seven coaches. Whilst clearing debris to get the coaches out, 'the smoke and heat were terrific. We found one fellow, apparently a garage hand, who had only started work at that garage that day, lying roasted. He had apparently been knocked out by the blast, pinned down by debris, and burnt alive whilst unconscious.'

London Transport's headquarters, 55 Broadway, did not escape bomb damage. This was the scene on the morning of 16 October 1940. *London Transport Museum*

Bill Maile was later commended for 'devotion to duty' and awarded a £5 cheque.

One of the first London Transport properties to sustain severe damage, despite being well to the west of most of the initial devastation, was Chiltern Court, the elegant flats built by the Metropolitan Railway above Baker Street station. The Secretary to the Board reported that on the raid of 9 September 1940, '55 flats were rendered uninhabitable'. On 18 February 1941 he reported that 'out of 144 flats at Chiltern Court not materially damaged by enemy action, 85 are empty: some of these had high minimum rentals and it is impossible to let them at the present time … Since air raids commenced, flat rentals in London have gone down.' The Secretary went on to report that the Estates Department had suggested letting some of the flats, 'on favourable terms, to officers of the Board' and this was agreed. The 55 damaged flats had some structural work carried out to maintain safety but remained empty for the duration and after the war were converted into offices. London Transport headquarters, 55 Broadway, was also bombed and a number of offices wrecked although there did not seem to have been any casualties.

It may seem extraordinary, but unexploded bombs from those days are still found in London. When I opened up the computer today, 1 May 2009, there headlined was the story of the discovery of a 2,200lb bomb turned over by a digger working on the site of the 2012 Olympics near Bromley-by-Bow Underground station. It was blown up and one was invited to watch the explosion on the screen of one's computer. I wonder what Londoners in 1940 would have thought of that?

A newspaper reported a typical raid on an unnamed East London borough in which 800 people were made homeless but only three were killed. It was reported that up to 5,000 people competed to see how many incendiary bomb fins could be delivered to the town hall, which was the sign of a bomb doused. The same borough had 25,800 houses and carried out 45,000 first-aid repairs and 42,000 secondary repairs, that is an average of four repairs for each house. Bomb sites, cleared of most of the rubble, were a feature of the London scene for decades after the war, one of the very last being on Ludgate Hill, just above the Circus which was still there, in 'temporary' use as a car park well into the 1960s. Bomb sites proved, you will not be surprised to learn, wonderful playgrounds for children, heedless, inevitably, of warnings to keep away. *Hue and Cry*, described as the 'first acknowledged Ealing comedy film', although it is more adventure than comedy, made in 1947, starred not only Alastair Sim and Jack Warner but a gang of 'bomb-site dwelling little cockneys' led by Harry Fowler, and made dramatic use of the numerous bomb sites around the Docks.

7

Sheltering in
the Underground

Animals instinctively dive for cover whenever danger threatens. People are no different, and an Underground shelter, more precisely a Tube station, seemed an ideal refuge to escape the Blitz. Which it was, although claustrophobia can be an equally powerful force, and the thought of being trapped underground is extremely frightening. But the exigencies of war force people into extreme measures. The authorities had, naturally enough, anticipated this. It is often forgotten that London suffered air raids during World War 1, mostly from Zeppelins although there was one raid by Gotha aircraft. The Gotha raid was particularly deadly, many people, including some on buses, being killed at Liverpool Street. Getting on for 200 people in all were killed in the raids, many injured, and damage caused over a wide area, ranging from Piccadilly to various suburbs. The Kaiser originally stipulated that civilian targets and historic buildings should be avoided, and the principal targets were, as initially during the Blitz, the London docks. In truth the airships were vulnerable to adverse weather conditions and mechanically unreliable, so the raids were relatively insignificant but they caused understandable panic, giving rise to notions that England might be invaded from the air. Thousands had sheltered in Tube stations and as the inevitability of war loomed in the late 1930s many East Enders' thoughts turned to repeating the exercise. London Transport knew that stations could not be occupied by both passengers and shelterers if the trains were still running, and in December 1939 notices were put up warning Londoners that in the event of air raids they must not use them as shelters.

Yet even before the Blitz began on 7 September 1940 the public had started to take up residence in the Tube at night. The *Ilford Recorder* published this account on 5 September 1940: 'Amazing scenes have been witnessed at Tube tunnels and subways, which have become something in the nature of human dormitories. As soon as the black-out hour arrives there begins a trek of scores of people who have no shelters. They take camp beds, blankets and food, cards and other games to while away the long hours.'

The *Recorder* reporter continued:

'I went to one of those subways just as a warning was sounded. I found that residents in the immediate vicinity had already "staked their claims" and were playing games, reading, knitting or sewing, according to taste. Easy chairs and deck chairs were displayed along one side, and on the opposite side camp beds and mattresses were laid down. It looked for all the world like a big dormitory.

'A Mr Green is a well-known "resident" of the shelter. Giving his account of how they work, he says: "At about half-past eight I gather my books and newspapers together and trot off to the shelter, where many other people are reading and playing games. The women, of course, do their knitting and sewing, and even darn. After I have read my paper I lean back and have my nightly talk with 'Mr Smith' on how we would run the war if we had charge. By the time the warning goes it's time for sleep, so I lie on my camp bed and go sound asleep to be wakened in the morning by a noisy alarm clock which does come in useful."

'At another construction site in the locality the doors were broken open by an excited crowd, and the police had to be called to restore order.'

But when the bombers did arrive, on 7 September 1940, thousands of East Enders, paying one and a half pennies, the cheapest possible Underground ticket, took up residence at various stations. And not just East Enders, for they came from further afield, the disused station at Southwark on the Northern Line even being taken over by coach parties and others who had arrived by car, complete with food, vacuum flasks and cooking stoves. As the evening wore on and the bombing continued thousands more headed into their nearest stations, all ages and conditions, breast-feeding mothers with their babies, children, young men and women, whole families, and the elderly. Many platforms became impassable to passengers attempting to alight at them and as soon as the last trains ceased to run the current was switched off and people moved on to the track. A great many of the shelterers made the best of the situation, entertained their children as well as they could, chatted amongst themselves and, eventually, attempted to sleep, but in truth it was pretty hellish with many of the elderly suffering from lack of fresh air, youths quarrelling and being general nuisances and the smell becoming steadily less bearable. Above all, nobody knew what they would find when the raids ended and they were able to emerge. The Mayor of Ilford, having gone down to the Tube station at Gants Hill to see conditions for himself, remarked, 'I would not stop a night there if anyone offered me £50 but apparently it suits quite a number of people.'

One might reasonably have thought that these remarks would not go down too well with the shelterers, but the Mayor was no idle speech-maker, rather a man of action and gave immediate instructions for improvements. 'Draught walls, gas curtains and bright lighting … caused a transformation', and when he returned 10 days later the shelterers, 'led by a woman who sang into a microphone … greeted the Mayoral Party with "For they are Jolly Good Fellows".'

In its edition of 20 September 1940 the *South London Press* reported that 'South Londoners, abandoning public overground and ground level shelters, are going underground every night in Tube stations causing the biggest crushes London Transport staff have ever seen … public shelters are almost deserted and early every evening queues of families with bedding and food stand in line four or five deep outside. Police have had to guard the doors since crowds have tried to rush the barriers as the sirens sounded, pushing back passengers trying to emerge.' Seven days later a reporter on the same paper described what he found at the Elephant & Castle, where the Bakerloo and Northern lines met. 'It took me a quarter of an hour to get from the station to the entrance to the platform. Even in the darkened booking hall I stumbled over bodies … going down the stairs I saw mothers feeding infants at the breast. Little boys and girls lay across their parents' bodies because there was no room on the winding stairs … Hundreds of men and women were partially undressed, while small boys and girls slumbered in the foetid atmosphere, absolutely naked. On every jutting beam and spike hung coats, waistcoats, shoes and shopping bags. On the platform, when a train came in, it had to be stopped in the tunnel while police and porters went along pushing in the feet and arms which overhung the line … On the train I sat opposite a pilot on leave. He looked dumbly at that amazing platform. "It's the same all the way along," was all he said. That night some 177,000 people in all spent the night sheltering in Tube stations.'

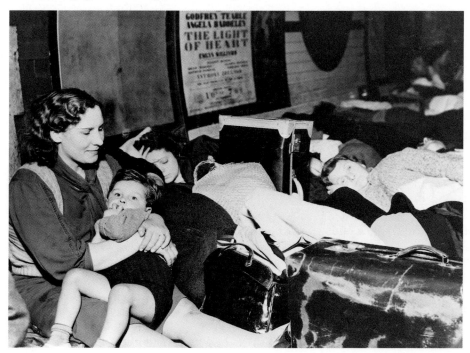

Night-time shelterers at Piccadilly Circus station in the autumn of 1940. There would seem to be very little room for people and luggage which they bring down each night. The play being advertised was one of Emlyn Williams' less successful efforts, its theme of a disabled daughter torn between caring for her famous, alcoholic father and her American lover perhaps having limited appeal in wartime. *London Transport Museum*

Women volunteers serve refreshments to shelterers at Holland Park Central Line station on 9 December 1940. *London Transport Museum*

Realising that there was no way people could be prevented from using the stations as shelters, London Transport set about organising the situation. And organise it did! Given that, unlike most of what London Transport had to deal with during the Blitz, there had been no preparations beforehand, it coped with remarkable alacrity and efficiency, even by its high standards.

Station staff had to stay on, voluntarily in many cases. Lighting had to be kept on. Normally there was only a gap of four hours between the last trains at night and the first next morning. Delays caused by air raids meant that this gap was often even less, and all the maintenance jobs, from cleaning platforms to electrical work, were affected. For a while London Transport had to cope unaided, but on 22 September 1940 stations were placed under Police supervision.

It was typical of the extraordinary attitude of just about every employee of London Transport from the Chairman to cleaners, porters, canteen staff etc that no difficulty would prevent a job which had to be done from being done just as quickly and efficiently as was humanly possible. Staff proved endlessly adaptable and if an initial system was seen not to work properly it was immediately modified until it did. Thus temporary first-aid posts and improvised lavatories appeared almost overnight, to be swiftly replaced by more permanent arrangements. Five inspectors had the responsibility of overseeing the immensely difficult but vital task of ensuring that hygiene and cleanliness prevailed. Thirty doctors and 200 nurses were employed. Their success was measured by the fact that the incidence of infection was one per 1,000 shelterers.

J. P. Thomas, who had retired from the post of General Manager of London Transport Railways, was appointed supremo to liaise between the Government, local authorities, and London Transport, a task he must have performed with great skill.

Stations being below main drainage level, chemical toilets had to be provided. Disposal was a huge problem, but with typical ingenuity a 'sewage-ejector plant' soon replaced manual labour. If you would care to know exactly how this worked, *The Railway Magazine* of September 1941 features a handy diagram, complete with 'manhole in drainage system', 'cut-off valve for overhaul' and a '200gal storage cylinder'. Phew!

The Ministry of Food asked London Transport to provide food on a regular basis for 150,000 people each evening. As *The Railway Magazine* commented, 'It would be difficult to find a place less suited to the service of refreshments than a tube-station platform.' There was no running water, no drainage and no naked flame was allowed so no cooking. Seventy-one stations were therefore equipped with water and electric power, the money for this being provided by the Lord Mayor of London's Air Raid Distress Fund. Tea cost 1d a cup (bring your own cup), milk for children one and a half old pennies; babies' bottles were warmed free of charge.

Special four-car Tube trains began work on 6 November 1940 delivering food, prepared at six railway depots, and packed in fibre, dust-proof containers. The trains set out at 1pm each day, stopping for just 30 seconds at each station to unload the food and collect the empties. Provision was made for distribution by road if rail service was interrupted. One thousand new employees had to be taken on and trained. Six women 'chosen for their interest in welfare work' — and, presumably, for their suitability to wear 'green frocks, red kerchiefs, rubber aprons and red armbands lettered "T.R." — were stationed at each feeding point. In winter they began work at 5.30pm, served refreshments between seven and nine o'clock, and by 10pm 'retired to their pneumatic mattresses'. They started work again at 5am and finished at 8am. For this they received six shillings a night plus food.

It made sense to direct as many people as possible to disused stations and sections of tunnel, such as the temporarily closed Aldwych branch or the as yet unopened Central Line east of Liverpool Street through Bethnal Green to Leytonstone. But of course these were only of use to those in the vicinity and within a few days 79 stations, each equipped with a medical aid post, had become the night-time home of Londoners, making a total of no less than 15 miles of tunnel and stations.

Highgate station did not open until 19 January 1941 but was in use as a shelter from the beginning of the Blitz and London Transport arranged that shelterers could travel there by train. The as yet uncompleted Central Line stations were ideal for use as shelters for there was no problem with trains running through them and, being close to the docklands area where the Blitz was at it its heaviest, they were in huge demand. An *Ilford Recorder* correspondent penned the following account for the issue of 19 September 1940:

'Nightly you see the pilgrimage from 5pm and in the case of temporarily homeless or those cases … where weariness or panic dictates, even into the night. Thus one morning at 3am, I saw a family come off a barrow which the pushers discarded on the middle green of the arterial road and stumble across to ask me nervously for the "Tube", I direct them their last half-mile having perforce been through almost continuous AA [anti-aircraft] fire to wait in a shelter for a lull before the last dash to the broad flights right-angled in the middle of Redbridge station workings. Platforms and concrete train track are there. Tunnels each way. Along one you could walk to Liverpool Street …

'The AA barrage continues … Splinters rain like hail on the house tops … Now I enter the shelter in a lull and beckon out the group quickly. A pair of brown eyes look up from a twelve-year-old who looks human and loveable just then … Otherwise, of course, a perfect little devil. A bus conductor whispers — the shelter is audibly asleep — "Look at my mate!" I look — he is asleep, standing against a post. Earlier he told me he drove home asleep.

'I lead them, chatting deliberately about their allotments and hobbies and families so they may recover their poise, to the yawning hole that is the Tube. Reaching the small tramway which the contractors used, and after one or two tired tumbles in the cement that abounds they carefully pick their way to the long, broad unfinished flight of steps down. A new flight at right angles brings them down to the dimly lit platforms. Moving figures in small groups. Darker and bigger masses lower down, all bedded down or in deckchairs, ordinary chairs, hammocks.

'On the right-hand side, sunken, is the railway trackbed some nine feet deep. Surely rats are moving about in the gloom down there. No, human beings — by the hundred. They lie at length under the platform overlap at any and every angle. Some sit with the tube curve for back support. All avoid actual contact with the channel way that has collected water at the bottom.

'Now we pick our steps, for it is darker and the feet of the sleepers meet, almost. They have parked for warmth and because space is valuable. We passed a small table illuminated and a paper sign that says "First Aid". A circle of chairs keeps it intact and operational. A very small group of "neighbours" (the word is coming back into its own) carry out this voluntary heroism.

"Is that the Home Guard?" A nearby voice, unidentifiable, low.

"Yes," quietly, and I halt my party by hand and arm contact. "What is it?"

"Is there any … any … news?"

"Yes, good news tonight. 163 down. Saint Paul's bomb, a ton in weight and found 27 feet down, safely carried on two lorries at top speed to Hackney Marshes and exploded in 100ft-wide crater. The Palace bombed. King and Queen safe."

'The Tube is alive! Voices and movements from the darkness. They are turning in their sleep? No, a brain cell keeps alert at all times and the news is spreading. You hear it taken up by countless voices in this "city of 2,000 sleepers".

"163," he says. "What, 163?"

"The Home Guard said so, 163 down."

"Wake up Jack, there's news, we're hitting back. Our boys are marvellous. They've brought down 163 (louder). What did we lose, sir?"

"We lost 30, but 10 pilots safe. Therefore eight to one, at least." '

Bunks were provided, sufficient for 22,000 people; the first supplied were wooden-framed, but it was soon realised that these housed vermin, so steel replacements followed. But bunks were not always the preferred option, for shelterers would arrive around teatime and would talk and socialise for several hours and this was not possible if bunks occupied most of the space. Notting Hill Gate pioneered a system which was universally adopted. Each shelterer was given a ticket with a number on it, this number indicating either a bunk or a platform space. A 6ft length of platform was sufficient for six people, three in a bunk, three sleeping on the platform in front of the bunk, whichever they chose. Some 10% of the platform space was held back for casual shelterers. This made life much easier for people who in the very early days of the Blitz might begin queueing quite early in the morning, whatever the weather, although no shelterer was allowed down into a station before 4pm. The relatively bright station lights on the platforms were dimmed at around 10 each night and restored at breakfast time. There were emergency hurricane lamps, volunteer shelter marshals and paid wardens at each station.

Regulation was certainly needed. As always, there were those who took advantage of other people's misfortune. Gangs of children demanded four pence for reserving platform space, for there were then, as now, plenty of dysfunctional families in inner London suburbs with children who either had been brought up, if that is quite the term one should use, in a criminal milieu or were simply out of parental control. Organised crime quickly moved in, in particular small-time tricksters, who had previously made a living reserving stools in the now closed theatre queues, and gangs demanded half a crown for platform space. They then dumped a few rags on the space until the families arrived. Not allowing anyone down on to the platforms did much to stamp out this racket.

The black market flourished during the war, for there were always those who could get their hands on scarce material and supplies, whether it was food, forged ration books, petrol, engine parts, just about anything. The 'spiv' quickly became a recognised figure and, like Hitler, was often turned in the media into a figure of fun. Arthur English, an excellent comedian, used to do a wonderful act based on a less-than-efficient wide boy; much later the character was reinvented, with James Beck as Private Walker in BBC TV's *Dad's Army*, whilst a distant relation of both was the immortal Del Boy of *Only Fools and Horses*. In reality the spiv, like Hitler, was a menace to society.

The other side of the coin was the efforts made by London Transport in association with other authorities and voluntary groups to provide shelterers with much more than the bare essentials. Play centres with qualified teachers were set up at the Elephant & Castle and Gloucester Road; there were 52 lending libraries, water fountains and cigarette machines were installed and at most stations committees were formed, some of which produced regular newspapers. The *Swiss Cottager*, if not typical, gives an insight to the quality of content some attained. Its clientele consisted of 'nightly companions, temporary cave dwellers, sleeping companions, somnambulists, snorers, chatterers and all who inhabit the Swiss Cottage station of the Bakerloo Line from dusk to dawn.' ENSA put on the first of a number of concerts at Aldwych station on 8 October 1940.

Christmas was not ignored, and at a meeting of the LPTB directors on 2 November 1941, Lord Ashfield asked the views of members as to whether the Board should provide special Christmas

UNDERGROUND RAILWAY STATIONS PROVIDE AIR RAID SHELTERS FOR THOUSANDS

decorations and toys for children at the stations used by the public as air raid shelters'. After discussion the decision was made that 'decorations similar to those erected last year should be provided at a cost not exceeding £500, but that toys for children should not be distributed having regard to the undesirability of attracting additional children to the station shelters at Christmas'. The *Ilford Recorder* of 26 December 1940 carried the following account:

'A stirring and unforgettable scene was presented at the children's party held on Saturday afternoon in a well-known tube shelter on the eastern outskirts of London.

Along the concrete levels, which will eventually become the station platform, long tables had been laid out for tea. The rather meagre and weird-looking electric lighting was helped out by many hurricane lamps standing every few feet along the tables.

Great coloured festoons, chains and balloons relieved the gloom of the vast spaces overhead, and the hurricane lamps illumined the paper caps of the children at the tea tables.

Down in the lower level where the electric rails will eventually be placed, men and women helped to prepare the food and wash the dishes.

A platform had been erected over a part of this long well, where a piano and a Punch and Judy show were accommodated, and best of all, a huge Christmas tree from which Father Christmas presented each child with a toy.

There were altogether 70 children entertained, including over 26 poor children from the Rev Tibbenham's parish at Plaistow. The latter were all brought and returned to their homes in charabanc parties.

The funds were raised by weekly collections among the shelterers while many gifts in kind were also received.'

A month earlier the paper had carried a report of the religious services held in the Tube shelters, 'braving shell fire on Sunday and Wednesday nights … believed to be unique in the suburbs'. They were run jointly by the Rev W. J. Redmore of the Eastern Avenue Methodist Church and a Jewish rabbi, Mr Smerditsky. The Rev Redmore commented: 'We have tried to get down there before the guns started firing but that has not been possible. As a matter of fact we go down when the guns are firing. It has been a little disconcerting, but one gets used to it. The presence of many Jews [remember this was the East End] makes it a little complicated, but they appreciate the services and they wish us to continue. It was, indeed, at the request of some that I went. I make my addresses as appropriate as I can to the times. At the first service I gave an address from Zachariah 8,13 — "Fear not, but let your hands be strong".'

In 1941, Arthur Askey and Richard Murdoch, two of the most popular comedians of the period (and for decades afterwards), starred in a film, *I Thank You*, which opens with Arthur, playing the part of an out-of-work actor, waking up 'next to a beautiful woman — no, two!' at Bank Underground station. Then there follows a sequence in which he plugs in his electric shaver (did you know such things existed in 1941?) to the train signal, but has to remove it when the light turns green and a train arrives and disgorges its passengers. Plenty of authentic posters, including one referring to tickets for sleeping places, adorn the platform walls. Singing away he completes his toilet, nearly stumbles over a recumbent figure who looks remarkably like Hitler and has the *Jewish Chronicle* by his side, and goes into the public phone box to ring Murdoch who says he's been trying to get him. Arthur explains that his doctor 'advised a change of air', hence him moving from his previous station. The film rattles on at a pretty breakneck pace, with all sorts of madcap adventures

which amused not only your author but also his five-and-a-half-year-old grandson, and ends with a grand singsong, at the station, which seems to have expanded considerably to accommodate all the cast, all about what they are going to do with Hitler when they catch him.

As for behaviour in air-raid shelters, a code gave the individual 'every liberty and the community every comfort'. However, liberty did not extend to 'spitting and throwing scraps of food on the floor'. Some inhabited their station for several months. Families whose homes were either destroyed or so badly damaged as to be uninhabitable, treated their nearest Underground station as their temporary home. London Bridge Northern Line station was the home of 350 people, 134 families, in the winter of 1940/1. Most made the best of it and, ironically, found themselves better off financially for they had no heating or lighting charges to pay, and hot drinks and a certain amount of food was provided, free of charge. They were surrounded by friends and were safe — probably.

Balham High Road, 15 October 1940. Civil Defence workers look down on LT669 which fell into the crater above the Tube station. *London Transport Museum*

Stations on surface lines, *i.e.* the Metropolitan, the District, the Circle and the East London, were more likely to suffer bomb damage than those serving the deep Tubes, but the latter were not totally immune from danger. On two successive nights, 12 and 13 October 1940, seven shelterers were killed in Trafalgar Square station and 19 at Bounds Green. Much worse was the bomb which hit Balham Northern Line station on the night of 14 October. It is also much the best remembered, certainly for the horrific deaths of the shelterers, but also for the picture of a double-deck bus embedded in the crater, an image reproduced time and again, worldwide. The raid also features in Ian McEwen's novel *Atonement* — wouldn't you just know it.

A few minutes after 8pm at the height of the raid a high-explosive 1,400kg armour-piercing fragmentation bomb fell in Balham High Road, directly above the station and exploded, fracturing a water main and a gas pipe. The bus, an LT from Shepherds Bush garage working route 88 towards Central London, in the words of the driver, 'began prancing about like a horse and the next thing I knew was that I was lying in a shop doorway'.

Down on the station, a motorman standing on the platform was aware of a terrific explosion above, causing a lamp to arc and the station to be plunged into darkness. There were some 500 people down on the platforms and panic ensued. The motorman, switching on his torch, saw water pouring down and realised 'it was time something was done to get these people out'. Opening an emergency hatch, in about 10 minutes he got between 70 and 80 people through it, then walked them up the escalator to the booking hall, where they were met by a rescue squad.

A photograph of Balham Northern Line station on the morning of 15 October 1940, showing the sand, sludge, sewage and water which cascaded onto the southbound platform after the water mains and sewage pipe were destroyed by the bomb, resulting in the death of 68 people. *London Transport Museum*

By now the water was pouring into the station, bringing with it torrents of sand and ballast. Another LT employee described it as 'like the sand and pebbles at Brighton on a very rough day'. The station was being filled up by this avalanche, trapping people beneath it, including the stationmaster and a booking clerk and his family. The LT employee — we're not told what his occupation was — decided to lead the Divisional Traffic Inspector and two policemen who appeared into the tunnel to see if anyone had taken refuge there and they headed through it towards the next station, Clapham South. They stepped off the platform into deep water, but our unknown hero was not worried ('I can swim') and led the way, carefully avoiding manhole covers and trip cocks, whilst all the time the water was getting deeper. Their only lighting was by torch. One of the policemen got his foot stuck in a check rail, which they struggled to free; 'it was only a couple of minutes but it seemed about ten.' The policeman was admonished and told to be careful and stay in line. Ahead they could see the lights of Clapham South station, but the water was now above waist height. Tube lines descend out of stations and rise towards them in order to help with acceleration and slowing down, but it was not until the water was chest high that the four reach the upward slope and safety.

The water was now so high that it has almost reached the lights, which would have caused a short and put them all out. They just managed to climb up on to the platform at Clapham South before the tunnel filled up. Well over 400 people managed to escape from the platforms at Balham, but between 65 and 68 — the precise number has never been confirmed — died. The enormity of this disaster was kept from the media, although there was no hiding it locally. The first bodies were brought out at around three in the morning, but the last were not recovered until December, more than eight weeks after the bomb fell, and the trains did not start running again until January 1941.

In a broadcast on the Home Service on 3 November 1940 the Minister of Home Security, Herbert Morrison, announced that a system of 10 new tunnels would be built, extended out from selected Tube stations, which would not conflict with the movement of trains but be capable of sheltering 100,000 persons, and that they would be completed by the autumn of 1941. In the event, with the lessening of the Nazi threat, they were not needed. After the war they were put to a variety of uses.

Not surprisingly, the extraordinary subterranean life down in the Underground attracted writers and official war artists, the most celebrated of these latter who produced images which have become embedded in the national culture being Henry Moore and John Piper.

The northbound platform at Balham with the debris almost touching the ceiling. The clock has stopped at two minutes past eight, the time the bomb fell.
London Transport Museum

8

29/30 December 1940

This was the night when the City of London came closer than on any other during the Blitz to complete destruction. That it didn't was down to a mixture of luck, weather and courage. Air raids had become almost a matter of routine and many families were temporarily re-united, evacuated children having come home for Christmas and not yet returned to the country. Unknown to them this was the night the Luftwaffe chose to try out a new, sophisticated guidance system which enabled its bombers to pinpoint their targets with great accuracy. The most extraordinary story to emerge from this terrible night was the survival of St Paul's Cathedral. Back in 1666, the old St Paul's succumbed with so much else in the city when human efforts proved no match for the firestorm which swept all before it. Christopher Wren's great church could so easily have suffered the same fate.

The raid began at 6.12pm. Walter Matthews, the Dean of St Paul's, takes up the story: '6.30pm — Incendiaries were landing over every roof and on the roofs of neighbouring buildings. All over the cathedral, small squads were now fighting separate battles. Some of the bombs were penetrating the lead sheeting, lodging in the roof timbers below. In half an hour, the scale of the attack was stretching our defences to the limit. 6.45pm — Though the dome was not yet on fire, the lead shell was beginning to melt. An incendiary was lodged halfway through the outer shell. We knew that, once a fire got hold of the dome's timbers at that high altitude, it would quickly be fanned into a roaring furnace. Unless it could be stamped out at the very start, the chances of the dome were slender indeed. Reporters had already cabled that St Paul's was in flames when the crisis suddenly passed. The bomb fell outwards into the Stone Gallery and was … put out. We thanked God our church was spared at the very moment the situation looked hopeless.'

Elsewhere the City was burning furiously. No fewer than 11,000 firebombs had fallen around St Paul's. Incendiary bombs could be extinguished if the firefighters could get to them quickly enough, but beyond a certain number the task was hopeless. This had happened when the RAF had bombed Munich after Churchill had decided that civilian populations near a military objective should 'feel the weight of war'. It was one of the disagreements Frank Pick had with Churchill. Germany had retaliated by bombing Coventry on 14 November 1940, killing 568 people and unleashing 150,000 incendiaries. Despite having firewatchers on its roof the defenders had been unable to save Coventry Cathedral, which today stands as an empty shell, alongside Sir Basil Spence's 1960s successor, and serves as a memorial to those who died, not just in Coventry but also in Dresden, the city with which Coventry is twinned.

After the Great Fire of London in 1666, Christopher Wren had planned a new city of wide streets, but the owners of the destroyed businesses were not prepared to wait, and rebuilt along the original, ancient, narrow streets. Their 20th-century descendants now paid the price for this impatience. The publishers, newspaper offices and works in and around Fleet Street contained, apart from vast amounts of newsprint, five million books. Every Victorian office building housed huge amounts of paperwork. Hitler must have thought his Christmases had all been rolled into this one night. The fires spread with terrifying speed, engulfing the Fleet Street area in less than 15 minutes. The livid red glow and clouds of smoke were visible for miles around.

The London Fire Brigade had encountered nothing like this before, yet still managed to film the scene, and newspaper reporters and photographers, many of them American, risked their lives to record the scene. In his book *Blitz — The Story of 29th December 1940* (Faber & Faber, 2005), M. J. Gaskin relates how William Lindsay White, an American correspondent, accompanied by a supporter of De Gaulle's Free French, eventually found a taxi driver who was prepared to take them into the City — not an easy task, as it was surrounded by a police cordon. But by showing their press passes they were allowed in and headed 'for the reddest area of the sky ahead.' By 9 o'clock every building in Paternoster Square was alight. So great was the heat that buildings literally exploded. In the words of 18-year-old firefighter George Wheeler, 'You'll see buildings not affected by the fire originally all of a sudden burst into flames. Then you realise: "Any moment this is going to jump, and St Paul's is going to catch fire".'

By 7.15pm some 200,000 people were sheltering wherever they could. Winston Churchill sent a message to the firemen: 'Save St Paul's.' He knew that the free world would see it as a symbol that London would survive. The Dean of St Paul's commented: 'We were grateful for this voice coming from the outside. But I cannot say it inspired us to greater effort. We were already working to the limit of human endurance.' Fire was all around them.

The hospitals were also working to their ultimate capacity and beyond. Down on the Embankment a tram, 'E1' No 1490, received a direct hit. Three people died, a number were injured and the bomb penetrated the District/Inner Circle Line below. Cannon Street, London Bridge — just one platform here remained operational — and Waterloo stations were all on fire. Ironically, until 1853 the site on which Cannon Street station had been built was the Rhenish Garden where German wines and beers could be sampled, Samuel Pepys being a regular customer. London Bridge and Waterloo stations were served by tram, as well as bus routes, which suffered also. Sixteen Underground stations were put out of action, no trains ran east of Temple. The section of railway along the arches between Waterloo and Clapham Junction was the most bombed stretch of line in London — or anywhere else in Britain for that matter — being hit 92 times between September 1940 and May 1941. Worse was to follow, for the firefighters began running out of water. The Germans had chosen their night carefully, a night when there was an exceptionally low tide on the Thames. The pumps clogged with mud and the fire crews had to drag their hoses across expanses of mud to reach the fireboats in midstream whence water could be pumped.

The two reporters watched a Wren church, St Bride's, burn. 'A black silhouette with light streaming from its windows. The smell of this fire was now all around us. Marguerite remarked how curious it was, not at all unpleasant but almost like incense or some very sophisticated perfume … It was the scent of the city of London burning.' St. Bride's, although badly damaged, survived and was restored.

Firefighter George Wheeler recalled that around 10pm '… suddenly you feel this burning wind hit you. And that is when the firestorm is starting up.' At Moorgate Underground station rails buckled and distorted from the intense heat and a District Line train was burned out. Remarkably a small section of this train still survives. One end of a P-stock motor car was salvaged and joined to the surviving end of a Q-stock trailer, the rest of which had been destroyed in a bombing incident at Plaistow, the 'new' motor car being numbered 14233. It now resides, deep in the countryside, at the Buckingham Railway Centre, better known to many as Quainton Road, which was once part of the Underground network, although never electrified.

Firemen at work in the City of London, December 1940.
Author's collection

London Transport may have had to deal only with mechanised vehicles but there were still many thousands of horses at work in London, millions nationwide, employed by the railways, by various street traders, and especially for the delivery of milk and bread. In October 1940, the Government had issued a directive which stipulated that 'From next Monday all horses must be securely tied during air raids [which] … will prevent roads being jammed by carts dragged by frightened horses.' A number of horses were trapped in the stables of a carrier, Suttons of Old Street, which was on fire and rescuers managed to get many, but not all, out. Firewatcher Stanley Champion had hold of one which was slipping on the road awash with water from hoses. M. J. Gaskin, in her *Blitz — The Story of 29th December 1940*, describes a sudden explosion resulting in Mr Champion's arms' being almost 'pulled out of their sockets' by the terrified horse.

Through this mayhem buses continued to run. The District Superintendent was getting reports of craters, etc all through the night from inspectors of where the bombs were falling. Normally 240 buses ran through the City each hour and just about every one of these had to be diverted. Many routes were turned round at such places as Liverpool Street, the Strand and London Bridge. A couple who lived in the Isle of Dogs attempted to get a train from Aldgate station but were told by a warden that none was running. They made for the nearest bus stop; two shot past without stopping but the third, bound for the Blackwall Tunnel, let them on board. The conductor refused to take their fares. Cannon Street station was out of action, and thousands of would-be passengers had to be taken home by bus and tram instead.

Because it was so important that every tram and trolleybus route be kept running if at all possible, the raids of 29/30 December ushered in a system whereby London Transport was given permission by various local authorities to demolish dangerous buildings which might well collapse and block thoroughfares. The tramway breakdown gangs were given this task. A steel hawser was tied around a section of the building, often the chimney stack, attached at the other end to a powerful lorry, quite often a converted bus. The building might come down after just one tug, sometimes it would need several, but down it would eventually come. If this work was being done the morning after a raid crowds would gather and give a cheer. The debris would quickly be cleared away and the trams or trolleybuses start running again.

St Paul's at the height of a bombing raid. *Author's collection*

By midnight the death toll amongst the firefighters had reached 12, and others were trapped, surrounded by burning buildings. One firefighter, Leonard Rosoman, an artist by profession, describes the death of a colleague. Rosoman had been working continuously for some seven to eight hours and was relieved by 'a rather quiet chap of about, I don't know, 19, 20, jokey and enthusiastic'. Rosoman and his senior officer left the alley where he had been tackling the fire and entered a warehouse to find a new vantage point for a hose. 'We were just about to mount the staircase when … a sound such as I have never heard in my life, which filled absolutely everything, every single inch … And then eventually tons of red-hot brick came down, with the fellow who'd come to take my place crushed to death at the bottom of it.'

Around the same time, notes the Dean of St Paul's, 'Fires were now raging on every side of the cathedral. We could see the wind carrying the flames from building to building. There were moments when six pails of water would have saved them, but there was no more water, and even if there had been, there were no more men to bring it.' A group of people approached St Paul's and asked to be let in. The Dean and others tried to persuade them that it was not safe, but '… they were frightened and distressed. Coming to the cathedral was somehow an act of faith.'

For the moment the bombers had gone but everyone knew they would be back, their aim being 'to prevent the firefighters from containing the inferno, to take the firestorm now building in the streets around St Paul's and carry it out into the city at large'. But as the night wore on, the firefighters began to make some sort of impression. In the words of 17-year-old Richard Holsgrove, 'If we could dampen down and keep the fire under control where we were, it wouldn't creep towards St Paul's. And bit by bit — although it was terrifying at the time — we started to control it.'

Above: An anti-aircraft gun firing during the Blitz in the winter of 1940. *Author's collection*

Opposite page: A demolition squad bringing down the remains of bomb-damaged buildings between Milton Street and Whitecross Street on the approach to Moorgate station on 5 February 1941. *London Transport Museum*

At 5am there was still no sign on the radar screens of the returning bombers. Just as the weather in 1588 had played into Sir Francis Drake's hands and helped destroy the Spanish Armada, just as a slackening of the wind on 5 September 1666 had finally enabled the firefighters to control the Fire of London, so weather conditions over Northern France had made it impossible for the German bombers to return and complete the destruction of the City of London. There would be many more terrible nights, but nothing quite on the scale of 29/30 December 1940.

The LPTB directors issued a statement the next day setting out the situation. Buses were using Tower Bridge, but they could not yet use London, Southwark or Blackfriars bridges, on account of the condition of the approach roads, although trams were able to negotiate the latter two. The Victoria Embankment tram services had been restored, as had trolleybuses on the Holborn Loop, but not to London Docks, Moorgate, or a section of the Whitechapel Road. Canning Town Bridge had been reopened, as had Silvertown Way. Opened in 1934, this was Britain's first flyover, carrying traffic into the heart of docklands. (One of the poles which supported the trolleybus overhead in Silvertown Way now performs the same task at the East Anglia Transport Museum at Carlton Colville in Suffolk, beside which two trolleybuses which regularly crossed the bridge still pass; the pole itself bears the scars of the Blitz with bullet holes and scoring from incendiaries.) Some 546 extra motor buses were in use covering sections of the Underground and tramways which were not operating. Around 103,600 people had spent the night sheltering in the Underground.

9
Coping with Hell

Amongst the preparations made in the days before the Blitz began was that of how to deal with the destruction of tram and trolleybus tracks and overhead wiring. This might mean diversions. Finding a way around bombed, impassable streets and roads for motor buses was far from easy, for the alternative might involve thoroughfares normally considered too narrow for two buses to pass; neither should the diversion take buses too far from the regular routes, for the general public still needed to be served. Finding an alternative for a trolleybus or tram service was very much more difficult, for it meant erecting temporary wiring and/or tracks. Sometimes the only solution was to substitute motor buses, but if the trams and trolleybuses with their greater capacity and their use of electricity rather than precious petrol or diesel could be got running again as soon as possible then this was done. A total of 216 men, working in teams of three, were employed as trolleybus linesmen and they performed miracles throughout the Blitz. In situations where the road was still passable, the average time taken from arriving at the scene to having the wires up and ready for the first trolleybus the next morning was an almost unbelievable four hours. And this might well be going on whilst the bombs were still falling. *The Passenger Transport Journal* of 14 April 1941 recorded an incident where 'working through the darkness with bombs still falling', trolleybuses were able to run right up to a crater which completely blocked the road. Later 'a detour of 500 yards … was planted with 43 poles, each six feet deep in the ground, complete with their overhead wiring within a few days of the bombing … a delayed-action bomb … also set back the work a little.'

The linesmen 'all agreed that the best repairs job was near a fire, as often happened', for the NFS (National Fire Service) pump 'drowned the noise of gunfire and the bombs … they kept warm as well'.

As for the trams, much agonising had already gone on in relation to ordinary maintenance. This was normally done at night, when the trams had ceased running, other road traffic was very light and digging up of the road and replacement of worn rails could be carried out. This, of course, required special lighting. Under wartime conditions this was clearly impossible; just imagine how gratified a Heinkel or Dornier bomb-aimer would have been to spot the brilliant flashes of light caused by electric arc welding. So the work was mainly transferred to daytime, chiefly at weekends when traffic was lighter and one line of a double-track stretch could be dealt with at a time. Where there had to be night work, particularly to repair bomb damage, then a screen was devised to cover any arc welding, with a peephole for the operator to see what he was doing. Emergency lights could be used, although obviously not whilst air-raid warnings were in operation.

A London Transport exhortation to trolleybus drivers.

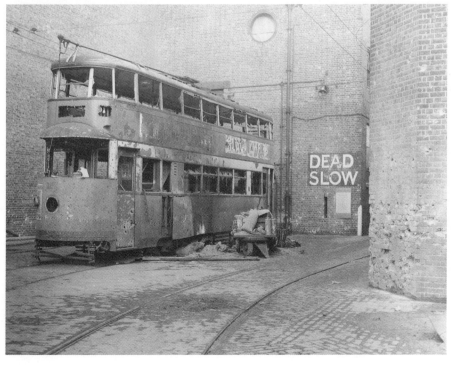

Above: Farringdon Street on the morning of 17 October 1940. The tramlines had not been used since route 17 was replaced on 6 March 1938 by trolleybus routes 517/617, but, as in most cases, the rails had simply been covered over with tarmac. Two tower wagons stand well back from the bomb crater, their crews ready to restore the trolleybus overhead as soon as possible. *London Transport Museum*

Left: 'Feltham' No 2152 at Charlton Works after being caught in the blast from a high-explosive bomb which dropped on the junction of Brixton Road and Stockwell Road on the night of 26 October 1940. The bodywork is pitted with shrapnel, the windows gone, the interior devastated, and although the structure appears basically intact the tram was a write-off. *London Transport Museum*

Kennington after a raid, October 1940. An LT manages to negotiate its way around the damage,
but in the distance trams can go no further for the time being. *London Transport Museum*

10

Survival and disaster on the Underground

For a long time I refused to travel on the Underground, for the simple reason that I had read and seen pictures of the results of bombs on different parts of the network and had a great fear of being trapped in the dark. I had good cause, for the system suffered grievously although, whilst services were disrupted from time to time, the staff performed miracles in restoring them and keeping trains running. One of my favourite outings — still is for that matter — was to the Science Museum. To get there we would take either the train or tram to Victoria and then the Inner Circle to South Kensington. The last part was a journey of just a few minutes with one intermediate station, Sloane Square. Shortly after one of our expeditions a bomb fell on it, on the night of 12 November 1940, causing some damage to a departing train and killing a number of waiting passengers and staff in the canteen. Because it was a station I knew, I felt personally threatened and from then on I would insist

we take a bus from Victoria, a 52, which was rather less convenient as we had to walk from its stop by the Albert Memorial down Exhibition Road.

The Sloane Square bomb might have caused even more devastation, for the Westbourne River is carried in a large pipe 15ft above the platforms on its way from the Serpentine to the Thames near Chelsea Bridge, making the station allegedly the only one in the world with a river running across it, and if that had been breached the station and the adjoining tunnels would have been flooded. It had only just been rebuilt, in March 1940, escalators replacing the 51 steps to street level. Until then it had been a real throwback to times past with gas lamps, aged framed advertisements, which had not changed since the days of steam trains, and a licensed buffet which at one time stayed open until one o'clock in the morning.

Sloane Square is, of course, in the West End, but inevitably it was the lines in the City and eastwards which suffered the most during the Blitz, as the

STL1404 on the forecourt of London Bridge station working an emergency wartime service to Moorgate in the autumn of 1940. A few days later the station was devastated by bombing, and much of the façade behind the STL and STD in the background destroyed. *Author's collection*

German bombers concentrated on the docks and the factories around them. The District Line depot at East Ham was frequently hit and 70 vehicles were damaged by a land mine. One of the earliest incidents took place at Plaistow on 7 September 1940 when one car of a stationary, empty train was blown on top of another. London Bridge main-line station was terribly knocked about on numerous occasions, some of which affected the Northern Line Underground station. Whitechapel, where the East London Line connected with the District and the Hammersmith & City lines was similarly targeted, the worst incident being on 10 May 1941, after which no trains were able to run between it and Bow Road for two days. Wapping, two stations to the south on the East London Line and right in the heart of the Docks, was destroyed by fire bombs on 11 September 1940.

Far and away the greatest loss of life on the Underground was sustained at Bethnal Green Central Line station on the evening of 3 March 1943, and by a bitter coincidence nine days later a bombing and strafing attack not far away, in Ilford, on a bus from Seven Kings garage, resulted in its total destruction and the death of the driver, this at a time when air raids were few and far between. The Bethnal Green tragedy was unlike any other, for it was outside the period of either the Blitz of 1940/1 or the missile attacks of 1944/5, the station was not used by trains, and the disaster was not caused, directly, by enemy action. Following his invasion of Russia Hitler had switched much of the Luftwaffe's activity to the Eastern Front, and raids on London tended to be confined to retaliatory sorties. A raid had been carried out by Bomber Command on Berlin on 1 March 1943, so Londoners were aware that retribution might be in the offing.

Temporary woodwork shores up the Metropolitan tracks at Kilburn & Brondesbury, as a compartment T-stock train gingerly crosses. *London Transport Museum*

Above: Modern 'Metadyne' stock looks somewhat incongruous, having been derailed by bomb damage to the track at Wembley Park, Metropolitan Line on 11 October 1940, but would appear to be undamaged. *London Transport Museum*

Left: Workmen pause to look at what appears to be an horrendous, not to say mammoth job of clearing the rubble at Mornington Crescent, Northern Line on 23 October 1940. Humphrey Lyttelton, who will forever be associated with the station which became an integral part of his Radio 4 quiz programme *I'm Sorry I Haven't a Clue*, was away fighting in North Africa. *London Transport Museum*

Turnham Green, District Line on 23 October 1940. The carriage is a clerestory motor car of 1910. *London Transport Museum*

As a general rule the media had to be sparing on what it reported, as far as precise details of location and casualties was concerned. The Government felt, probably rightly, that too much graphic horror, military setbacks and high numbers of casualties would affect morale, although, not surprisingly, editors and reporters were irked by censorship, and readers and wireless listeners learned to read between the lines and deduce what might have happened and where. Then again, some new weapon might have been used and the less said about it the less the enemy would know. The Bethnal Green disaster resulted from an incident in the second category.

There had been 10 air-raid warnings that evening; by now East Enders were well used to the whine of the siren and would have to make up their minds whether to carry on regardless, or head for a shelter,

either their own Anderson, a communal purpose-built one, or down into the Underground. Bethnal Green, the first station east of Liverpool Street, should have been serving Central Line Tube trains but war broke out before the route from Liverpool Street on to Stratford, Woodford, Epping and Ongar could be opened, leaving much of it still worked by LNER steam trains. Instead the virtually complete station became an air-raid shelter with a capacity of several hundred and would not start to serve its intended function until 4 December 1946. At the height of the Blitz it had been packed every night, but by 1943 numbers were generally far fewer. The air-raid siren sounded at 8.17pm, and people began to head for the shelter; 500 were already inside. People came out of local cinemas, three buses stopped, and the cinema-goers and bus passengers joined those making for the shelter. Suddenly, at 8.27pm, there was the most tremendous noise, and the crowd (which until then had been walking, not running), now assuming that bombs were falling close by, began to hurry down the steps, the only entrance to the station. The entrance was narrow, there was no handrail, and it was dark, restrictions on lighting meaning that a single 25W bulb had to suffice; it had also been raining, and the steps were wet. Near the foot of the steps a woman carrying a baby slipped. An elderly man tripped over her and also fell. Within 15 seconds dozens and dozens of others had piled up on top of them. Tragically, 173 (some sources say 172) perished.

Schoolboy Alf Morris was a survivor. 'It's indescribable what went on in them few minutes when most of the people died … the screaming, the hollering.' Another survivor was James Hunt. 'When I arrived here there were all the bodies laid right the way down. I helped to get some of the youngsters up, I was only little myself, I picked up mostly young children.' Alf Morris, interviewed in May 2009, described how a woman, Maude Chumbley, had rescued him. 'First of all she grabbed me hair — "Gotcha!", she went, and she pulled. She could see

that I couldn't get out so then she put her arms under my armpits and lifted me out.' Mr Morris is one of the organisers of the Stairway to Heaven campaign which is raising money for a permanent memorial — there is presently only a plaque at the station — to those who died. He eventually managed to make contact with Maude Chumbley's granddaughter, Susan Lane, and met her outside the station. 'I just couldn't believe it that somebody had remembered my nana. I've always been proud of her — she's always been special.'

A newspaper reporter, Eric Linden, filed the story of the tragedy for the *Daily Mail*; it was never published. The Government was accused of censoring the story, although *The Times* published an account but without mentioning the location. This was common practice during the war, a somewhat

Clearing the debris at Sloane Square District and Circle Line station after the direct hit of 12 November 1940, which killed 79 passengers. *London Transport Museum*

farcical one, for local papers covering a very precise area would have to limit themselves to referring to 'an incident in an area of (say) south-east London', and then go on to mention names and addresses of those involved. The official line at first was that there had been a direct hit by a bomb on the station and later, admitting that there had been panic, that this had been caused by enemy aircraft overhead. An inquiry was held, but its results were not made public until after the war. This inquiry found that the lack of a crash barrier, poor lighting and inadequate supervision by either the Police or the ARP had all contributed to the disaster.

What had caused the 'deafening roar' and the subsequent panic was not, ironically, any direct enemy action but a new form of anti-aircraft rocket being tested in nearby Victoria Park by a military Z-Battery unit. It has proved impossible to precisely pin down why local people were not given some sort of warning, despite surviving members of other such units expressing surprise that this was not done. Alec Allen, a young man who worked as a 'cocoa boy' (general dogsbody) for one such unit, claims that he was told by his commander that tests were to be carried out that night. Another described the firing of such a weapon as, 'It was as if all hell had been let loose, belching out flame and noise as you've never heard.'

The death toll was the worst single wartime incident anywhere in the London area, and the greatest loss of life there has ever been on the Underground.

Devastation at Moorgate on 31 December 1940, with an almost new P-stock motor car burnt-out in the midst of the carnage. *London Transport Museum*

11

Business as usual

espite the upheavals which war brought to London Transport, normality was never far away. A good place to look for this is in the reports of meetings of the Board of Directors. On 4 May 1944 there is a reference to 'strikes which occurred at certain Bus Garages and Trolleybus Depots from the 19th to the 22nd April 1944, in connection with the introduction of the summer schedules'. At the same meeting the General Manager 'submitted a report setting out the receipts and expenses incurred in connection with the Lost Property office for the year ... together with statistics of the articles received and claimed'. £50 was to be spent, as in previous years, on the Station Gardens Competition. Rather more was authorised on 2 October 1941, £2,000 in fact, 'for the provision of music and entertainment for the staff employed in the Board's Works at Chiswick, Charlton and Acton'.

A rather curious item is that discussed at some length on the first day of 1942. Back in August 1939, Major I. F. MacAlpine, a Divisional Superintendent (Central Buses), 'had approached the Board for financial assistance'. In line with long-standing practice, 'subject to repayment (with interest) and to satisfactory security', the Major was loaned £1,067, a considerable sum. However, in May 1940, the Major left the employ of London Transport and resumed his army career, 'since when the repayments have not been fully maintained'. Seemingly in no way disconcerted by this the Major had again approached the Chairman for 'further financial assistance, owing to his being pressed by his creditors.' Hardly surprisingly, it was resolved that 'no further financial assistance be granted to Major MacAlpine'.

At the next meeting, the subject of loans to staff was again aired. Members were informed that: 'Since 1924 it has been the custom of certain undertakings now merged with the Board to grant loans to

Two motor cycle combination despatch riders, the one on the right wearing an overcoat which would not have looked out of place on an RAF bomber pilot, at Camberwell garage on 22 April 1940. *London Transport Museum*

Right: Following the Japanese conquest of Malaya and the surrender at Singapore, 90% of the UK's rubber supplies were in enemy hands. Thus every effort was made to make tyres last as long as possible. In this picture, taken at Chiswick Works on 26 November 1942, a London Transport employee is removing a tyre which has just been remoulded and is 'now good for about 30,000 miles' according to the LT caption of the time. *London Transport Museum*

Below right: Even bus horns made of rubber had to be given up for salvage, and in this picture, taken on 19 October 1942, 'A workman of the LPTB is making substitutes for the rubber section of the motor horns, out of scrap material'. *London Transport Museum*

members of the clerical staff in necessitous cases, and that this practice has been continued by the Board … At present there are only 13 cases outstanding and the majority of these were made on account of family circumstances.' The total outstanding on these 13 came to £379 and 'up to the present there had been no case of failure to repay'. Clearly the Major was very much the exception to the rule.

On 17 May 1940, Frank Pick, the Vice-Chairman and Chief Executive Officer of the LPTB resigned and became Director of the Ministry of Information. It has been suggested that he and Lord Ashfield had fallen out, but one wonders if this was really so, for they had worked together for over 30 years, forging a relationship which had proved of inestimable value to London Transport and its combine predecessor. More than anyone else, Pick was responsible for the unique status which London Transport enjoyed, being generally recognised as the finest city transport authority of any size, worldwide. The minutes recorded that: 'It was unanimously RESOLVED to record the Board's deep appreciation of the great work which Mr. Frank Pick had carried out during his 34 years' service with the Underground Group of Companies and the Board … and to record their very sincere regret at the loss of his most valuable services.' A little over a year later Pick was dead. Just eight lines in the minutes of 4 December 1941 record

A meeting of the Board of5London Transport in April 1940 in the disused Dover Street Tube station. Frank Pick is on the far right. The picture must have been the last taken of him as a member of the Board, for shortly afterwards he resigned to take up the government post of Director of Information but sadly died a year later. *London Transport Museum*

vthe event, it being resolved that the Secretary should 'convey, on behalf of the Board, their sincere sympathy to Mrs Pick and members of the family in the loss which they have sustained'. Given that Frank Pick, a solicitor by trade, born in Lincolnshire in 1878 was, in the words of Sir Nikolaus Pevsner, 'the greatest patron of the arts whom this century has so far produced in England', was first Chairman of the Council for Art and Industry, later the Arts Council, advised foreign governments on constructing underground networks, being awarded an honorary badge of merit by Josef Stalin — with whom there could not have been a greater contrast — for his work on the Moscow Metro, commissioned the greatest artists of the day to design buildings, posters, maps, including the iconic network diagram by Harry Beck, which set a world standard, as well as championing the expansion of the Underground network with stations which would reflect the modern, progressive spirit, yet refused all honours, it seems (to put it mildly) a mealy-mouthed tribute to a towering genius, without whom London Transport would never again scale the heights to which he had led it.

Perhaps Pick's departure from London Transport had not been totally amicable, but the truth was that Pick had standards from which he refused to budge, even offering to resign when several members of the Board looked like buckling to those who objected to Jacob Epstein's monumental figures on the façade of the LPTB's headquarters at 55 Broadway. He also clashed with some of the politicians with whom he had to deal in his new post, notably with Winston Churchill over the use of propaganda. Churchill felt that no holds should be barred in terms of what should be promulgated when the very existence of the country was at stake, but for Pick there were boundaries over which he would not step. It was a sad but not unpredictable end to a glittering career, but he left London Transport fit to overcome the unprecedented trials of the 1939-45 years, and his influence is still all around us.

The cursory manner in which Pick's retirement and subsequent death are recorded contrasts greatly with that of T. E. Thomas CBE, who retired in the autumn of 1945. A whole page of the minutes is devoted to his achievements, beginning with his service with the London United Tramways, starting in 1899 when horse traction ruled, his transfer to the publicity and commercial section of the Underground Group, where he was Commercial Assistant to Frank Pick, then being put in charge of all trams and trolleybuses when London Transport came into existence in 1933, rising yet higher in 1939 by which time he was responsible for the operation of all the undertaking's buses, trams, trolleybuses and trains, and finally becoming General Manager of London Transport in 1943.

Various reports brought out during the war years looked to the future, assuming it would be controlled from Westminster rather than Berlin, such as

The cover of a booklet produced by the *Evening News* showing various London streets and buildings before and after the Blitz. *Author's collection*

'London Replanned — Interim Report of the Royal Academy Planning Committee', and the very influential 'Abercrombie Report', as it came to be known, officially the 1943 County of London Plan, leading to the Greater London Plan of 1944.

In 1941 the Minister of Works had asked the London County Council to look to the future, and what ultimately emerged under Patrick Abercrombie, a planner described as 'the only philosophic and/or sociological planner in the country … the recognised head of the profession' (a quote from Frederick J. Osborn, very much involved with the Town & Country Planning Association, who before the war had worked on Letchworth and Welwyn Garden City and would afterwards work on the New Towns) was that the devastation wrought during the Blitz could be turned to advantage. In the words of Viscount Samuel, 'The destruction of parts of our cities brings with it some compensation in the opportunities opened.' Essentially the Greater London Plan envisaged people moving away from Central London and into and beyond the suburbs, to a ring of new towns. London would be divided into four rings — Inner, Suburban, Green Belt and Outer Country. Eastwards this would include Brentwood and Billericay, north to Bedford, Luton, Basildon and Harlow, north-west to High Wycombe, south to Farnham and Sevenoaks. The implications for public transport were profound and not particularly encouraging.

It was proposed that a number of ring roads would encircle London, involving considerable demolition of property. This was based, to a degree, on a Ministry of Transport report of 1937 by Sir Charles Bressey and Sir Edwin Lutyens. There was no doubt that such plans were essential, not only to deal with the aftermath of the bombing of London but also the longer-term problems of overcrowding, slum conditions and narrow streets unsuitable for modern traffic. A good deal of what was proposed came to pass; quite a lot didn't. The intentions were honourable and sympathetic to the people of London but, perhaps inevitably, the crystal ball was distinctly cloudy; much that lay in the future, particularly the need to control the extraordinary demand for space for airports as we moved into an era in which air travel became a universal experience, and, even more vital, the need to place restrictions on just where and when the private motor car could be allowed, was not foreseen.

12

Country affairs

Two of the more astonishing statistics relating to the war concern the Country Area. By August 1945 the mileage covered by the 'green' buses (some of which were actually painted red, but we'll put that aside for the moment) was 32% higher than in 1939, whilst even more remarkable was the fact that the number of passengers carried had almost doubled, 90% to be precise. These increases explain why some of the Country Area buses were red: there weren't enough green ones. The only double-deckers built new by London Transport for Country Area service before 1939 had been two batches of forward-entrance STLs, 139 in all. The rest of the double-deck fleet consisted of STs, the 12 lowbridge 'Godstone' STLs, various elderly Leyland Titans and the experimental Q and LT coach. In 1939 39 new, FJJ/FXT-registered, standard roofbox STLs were sent to the Country Area, prompting the question why had it ever been necessary to build the forward-entrance examples in the first place? These

latter had their seating capacity increased from 48 to 52 by removing luggage space.

It will be recalled that Green Line services, after initial withdrawal on the outbreak of war, soon reappeared, but some two years later, to quote the General Manager (Operations), 'In view of the urgent need for economy in the use of motor fuel and rubber for tyres, the Minister of War Transport has directed that the Green Line Coach Services of the Board should be withdrawn on and from 30 September 1942 on the understanding that where the withdrawal of the coaches would leave roads unprovided with bus facilities, existing bus services should be strengthened or extended in replacement of the withdrawn coach services.' This was a direct result of the Japanese conquest of Malaya and Singapore, which Winston Churchill in February 1942, giving the news to Parliament, described as 'the worst disaster and largest capitulation in British history'. It meant we had lost 90% of our rubber supplies and petrol was now even

Central Area STL1147, with several boarded-up windows, at the Tunbridge Wells terminus of temporary Green Line service 5, sometime in 1941. *Author's collection*

harder to come by. At a meeting of the Board on 1 October the Chairman 'expressed regret at [this] enforced withdrawal … and congratulated the General Manager (Country Buses and Coaches) and his staff on the work they had done over many years'.

In all Green Line had operated 33 services between December 1940 and September 1942, as under.

2	Victoria–Gravesend
3	Victoria–Wrotham
5	Victoria–Tunbridge Wells
8	Victoria–East Grinstead
9	Oxford Circus–Crawley
10	Oxford Circus–Reigate
14	Victoria–Epsom–Dorking
15	Victoria–Kingston–Dorking
18	Oxford Circus–Guildford
20	Victoria–Chertsey
21	Victoria–Staines
23	Victoria–Ascot
23A	Victoria–Sunningdale
26	Victoria–Windsor
26A	Victoria–Farnham Common
33	Oxford Circus–High Wycombe
34	Oxford Circus–Amersham–Chesham
35	Victoria–Wendover–Aylesbury
40	Victoria–Berkhamsted–Aylesbury
40A	Victoria–Hemel Hempstead
40B	Victoria–Watford
45	Victoria–Radlett–Luton
46	Victoria–Barnet–Luton
47	Victoria–Hitchin
47A	Victoria–Welwyn Garden City
49	Oxford Circus–Hertford
52	Oxford Circus–Epping
53	Aldgate–Bishop's Stortford
54	Aldgate–Eastern Avenue–Romford
55	Aldgate–Romford–Brentwood
58	Aldgate–Corbets Tey
59	Aldgate–Chandlers Corner–Grays
59A	Aldgate–Aveley–Grays

Double-deck buses had performed much of the Green Line work between 1939 and 1942, and these stayed on in the Country Area, being joined by 75 more STLs, diverted from the Central Area and painted green. Even this was insufficient and some 225 more were transferred in the next three years. This time they retained their red, or, in some cases, austerity brown livery, although eventually all received green. The attractive prewar Country Area livery of two shades of green, with black lining and silver roof gave way to dark green and white, with roofs painted either grey or brown. Many of the STLs were put to work on routes which had formerly been the preserve of single-deckers, and where this was not possible because of low bridges or overhanging trees, the frequency was increased. It is worth noting that the side-engined Q class, despite being of a largely untried, semi-experimental design, performed yeoman service throughout the war and for a number of years afterwards.

Examples of routes which had their Green Line services replaced by Country Area buses were between Epping and Bishop's Stortford, between Bromley and Tonbridge, where the half-hourly 402 service is still, incidentally, operating today, was considered by transport historian John Price 'somewhat in excess of requirements', and the 443 between Staines and Ascot. The STLs operating this latter 'gave you one of the fastest and most exhilarating rides in the London area, the bus being invariably driven flat out for several miles', in the words of John Price. The relative absence of other traffic during the war meant buses, particularly in the Country Area, could make almost unimpeded progress. London buses had no speedometers in those days; I once asked the driver of preserved STL2377 how he coped with this and he said, 'I simply keep up with everyone else.'

One of the reasons for the huge increase in bus travel in the Country Area was the number of war industries it served. Dartford, for instance, had several and the number of buses allocated to Dartford garage far outstripped its capacity and, as at several other garages, the surplus buses were parked on rented cinder patches. Factories involved in war work could be found all over the Country Area, one of the most important being that of Vickers at Weybridge and its various satellites, and to serve these the T- and LT-class single-deckers based at Addlestone garage were painted grey to make them less conspicuous from the air, as were some Leatherhead- and Sutton-based buses.

It was at the Cobham outstation of the Vickers Works (at the time of writing the home of the London Bus Preservation Trust) that Dr Barnes Wallis conducted his experiments with the bouncing bomb. Many of his initial trials were held on Silver Mere, before he moved on to try out a full-size dummy bomb off Chesil Beach, Portland in Dorset. David Kinnear, Curator of Cobham Bus Museum, relates an amusing story concerning Dr Wallis and Sir George Edwards, celebrated aircraft engineer and

Sevenoaks bus station in early 1940. Former Green Line T286, now serving as a Country Area bus from Dunton Green garage, with a forward-entrance STL behind. Both vehicles would appear still to be in prewar livery with the addition of white-painted mudguards. *Author's collection*

Another view of Sevenoaks in early 1940 with, from left, a Maidstone & District lowbridge Titan TD4, STL1465, still in prewar two shades of green livery, a slightly later, ELP-registered STL on the 403ʙ to Tunbridge Wells and an elderly Bedford belonging to an independent operator. *G. Robbins collection*

Manager of the Experimental Department of Vickers Armstrong. One day in 1942 Sir George was standing on the shore of the lake, watching the great man wrestling with a home-made wooden catapult, shooting various-size balls made of different materials and which he retrieved, where possible, by a rowing boat. After a while Sir George, who was a passionate cricketer, said to him: "Dr Wallis, it is evident you don't play cricket." Dr Wallis, in his boffinish way, retorted: "Well, Edwards, I can't imagine how you arrive at that conclusion …" Sir George replied: "Well, if you did, you would remember that to get a man out you have to bowl him a 'googly'. One uses backspin to make the ball stand up in front of him. I note your catapult is firing topspin. Why don't you get it to make the marble go round the other way?" Dr Wallis said it sounded like a preposterous hypothesis,

but he would, nevertheless, try it. Sir George was duly proved right, and the marble sprang up on hitting the water, the experiment leading to the famous WW2 raid on the Ruhr dams.

Despite the war, London Transport brought out summer timetables each year and that beginning on 2 April 1941 contained a number of alterations to Country Area routes, which illustrate the increasing demand for its services. For instance, between Barnet and Hitchin the frequency of the 303/303ᴀ was doubled and double-deckers replaced single-deckers, Cubs were taken off the Hertford-based 389 and 390 routes and replaced by 30-seat Ts, and, in the southern area, increasing use of the 418 saw it extended so that it ran all the way from Kingston to Guildford, replacing the 432, which had previously covered part of the route.

Right: Barnes Wallis, the inventor of the 'bouncing bomb', who carried out much of his experimentation at one of the outstations of the Vickers aircraft factory, Cobham, now the home of the London Bus Preservation Trust. *Author's collection*

Below: Kingsbury Square, Aylesbury, pictured on 7 March 1945. On the left can be seen two coaches, the leading one a Dennis Lancet on its way to Halton Camp, whilst on the right is a Country Area ST about to set off for Watford on route 301. *London Transport Museum*

13

1941

After the appalling destruction of 29/30 December 1940, the first 10 days of 1941 were relatively quiet but, on Saturday 11 January, the Luftwaffe unleashed more mayhem. The LPTB directors reported: 'During the Saturday night raid, Green Park, St Paul's, Baker Street and Bank stations were damaged, the latter station being severely damaged. There were fatal casualties at these stations both to staff and to members of the public, but the details of these casualties are not yet available. It is practicable to use the stations for traffic as the damage does not interfere with the running of trains, but it has been necessary to close Hyde Park Corner station owing to an unexploded bomb in the vicinity, which has also necessitated the closing of the running tunnels.

'In addition there were intermittent interruptions of the train services, particularly on Saturday night, due to incendiary and HE bombs, but the services were generally restored within a comparatively short while.

'On the roads on Saturday night 15 buses were damaged, four of them severely; these four buses were in Bishopsgate; two drivers and one conductor were killed and one driver and two conductors injured, and, as far as is at present known, 22 passengers were killed and others injured. The remaining 11 buses sustained minor damage, mainly broken windows, and in these incidents one driver and two conductors sustained minor injury.

'Also on Saturday night, the upper saloon of one tram at Brockley was burnt out by an incendiary bomb and one other tram and two trolleybuses had windows blown out. Elephant & Castle Tramway Substation suffered damage to the roof and windows, but there was no interference with current supply, and at Brixton Tramway Substation there was a slight fire, which caused a failure of current for about an hour. On Sunday night, three trolleybuses sustained minor damage, mainly to windows, and two conductors were slightly injured.

'The position upon the road services is, of course, rather worse, particularly in the City area, although the opening of Blackfriars Bridge and Bishopsgate this morning had somewhat improved the position for the bus services; the closing of Knightsbridge is affecting West End services. On the trams there are a number of cases where the services have been broken due to track damage at Brixton Hill, at Blackfriars, in Old Kent Road and St George's Road; an unexploded bomb in Brighton Road, Croydon, has caused a break in the through tram services and in a number of other instances overhead tram and trolleybus wires were brought down but have been replaced.

'The number of buses provided this morning for special services is 228, additional vehicles having been provided to meet the closing of the Piccadilly Line and for the replacement of services upon the Southern, and London, Midland & Scottish Railway.

'The floodgates on the under-river sections were closed at 6.20pm on Saturday and reopened at 11.39pm and closed on Sunday at 6.29pm and reopened at 10.52pm.

'The number of shelterers in the Tube stations on Saturday night was roundly 97,000 and on Sunday 91,000; it was necessary to evacuate the shelterers from Hyde Park Corner station on Saturday night, and these shelterers were transferred to other stations.'

The worst incident that night took place one minute before 8pm at Bank station. A bomb crashed through the roadway and the Central Line concourse and exploded in the escalator machine room. The blast went down the escalator shaft, hurling passengers at the bottom of the escalator and standing on the platforms against the opposite wall. Although the Board of Directors' initial report does not give casualties, it was later determined that 56 died and 69 were badly hurt. The flood doors were open, had they been shut the Civil Defence were of the opinion that the blast might well have smashed the tunnel walls apart. An enormous crater, 120ft by

100ft, was created. First on the scene was a rescue party from Liverpool Street, who had to work without lighting, other than the oil lamps, hand-lamps and candles they themselves carried. They were quickly followed by doctors and nurses from nearby St Bart's hospital. A train was actually entering the station when the bomb fell; the motorman's hands were blown off his controls but the automatic brake stopped the train, however, not before several shelterers who had been blown on the track were run over. Within three hours all the bodies had been removed except for a number trapped beneath the escalators. One member of staff who was taken, injured, to Bart's hospital had been blown clear and was discovered wandering about not knowing what had happened.

A driver of a double-deck bus with many Auxiliary Fire Service personnel and Police aboard working route 21 from Farningham to Moorgate describes what happened when he reached King William Street: 'I suddenly saw a cloud of dust and smoke, heard a terrific crash, and then I saw in front of me a big crater, and felt the bus sink beneath me. I had immediately applied my brakes, but it happened so suddenly I wondered what to do.

'I looked round and saw my conductor was still OK. The next person I saw was a soldier, and he and my conductor with others formed a chain and helped me out of my cabin. The front of the bus was hanging over the crater, and had a broken axle. I have since learned that 111 people were killed in the shelter under the roadway where the bomb fell.

'Whilst standing there another stick of bombs fell and we lay in the gutter for a few minutes.' Eventually he and his conductor made their way back 'as best we could' to their garage and reported

Aerial view of the devastation at Bank Tube station after the high-explosive bomb which exploded in the booking hall on 10 January 1941. Estimates of the number killed vary, but it was around 111; the Government, as in a number of other incidents with a large number of casualties, tried to keep details out of the media. *London Transport Museum*

'Breakdown owing to enemy action.' Bank station was out of operation for two months.

In some respects the night of 10/11 May 1941 was the worst of all. The raid began half an hour after midnight with 168 bombers coming in over the Thames, followed by another 100 aircraft 30 minutes later. Less concentrated than the raids which so nearly destroyed St Paul's Cathedral, this one covered a much greater area although, as always, the East End and the City suffered the most. In all, 1,486 people were killed and 11,000 houses were destroyed. The Houses of Parliament, the British Museum, the Queen's Hall, home of Sir Henry Wood's Promenade Concerts, were all hit, the latter burned to the ground. A large number of buses, trams, trolleybuses and Underground trains were damaged. There were 20 direct hits on the Underground system, and in four places tunnels caved in. At Baker Street station a guard described how his supper was interrupted when incendiaries fell on the station and how by the time they had been put out … 'I went back to finish my supper but found it was spoilt and the tea cold.' Later … 'I walked up the main-entrance stairs and a sight met my eyes over in the distance. It was as bright as day. The sky was a deep red from the fires that burned

So devastating was the Bank Underground station bomb that two months later, on 15 March 1941, restoration work was still ongoing. A Bluebird LT is crossing the temporary bridge whilst work continues below. *London Transport Museum*

… I was looking towards a fire that was burning on the top storeys of Bickenhall Mansions, when I heard a whistle getting nearer, and one of the chaps up there shouted, "Look out, bomb coming down!"… I was looking for a place when the bang came. My ears seemed to be bursting and it felt like a hot wind on my face. Then something seemed to be tugging at me; then I dropped flat on the floor. A glass window fell with a crash not very far from me. The lights went out, then up again; dust came down in clouds as I lay there … the All Clear did not go up until about 6 o'clock … what a mess. Glass and woodwork all over the place, and dust. I've never seen such a lot before. I never want another night as that.'

A driver of a Circle Line train described what happened at Aldgate station: 'There was terrific gunfire and bombs bursting … I was about two coaches' length away when the bomb fell … The bomb smashed my cabin. The only effect I felt was in my ears. I seemed to go temporarily deaf, but it passed off quickly. It left a ringing in my ears which lasted for a month afterwards … We had three men passengers who had had a few drinks. They were awkward drunks and we tried to send them out of the way but they wouldn't have any of it. They would stay with us; they felt safer. Incendiaries fell on the bridge and we helped to put them out. One drunk helped us to put them out and he made a good job of it. After the H.E. bombs dropped we never saw any more of them. I think it put the wind up them and they cleared off … I was saying to myself that I didn't think I would get home in the morning. I felt it was my last time. I made up my mind I was fated. It seemed so terrific; if you weren't killed, the bomb blast would kill you. I just carried on, though. But I don't feel so confident now as I did.' Carrying on in such circumstances has always seemed to me the highest form of bravery, worthy of both the Victoria and the George crosses.

This was the night Croydon garage was hit. Bombs fell on Croydon over a period of seven hours, the raids only ending at daybreak. The area most hit was that around the Red Deer where the garage was and, indeed, still is situated. Croydon garage had not dispersed its vehicles. It was certainly not unique in this, but it is said that they were all inside the garage because residents in the streets nearby where they might have been parked were worried that the lights used to clean the vehicles by would attract bombers.

As it happened a huge blaze at a nearby varnish factory acted like a beacon. Two bombs hit the garage. W. C. Berwick Sayers, Croydon's Chief Librarian during the war, recorded, 'There were men inside, some of whom, when the first bomb fell, had dived into one of the examination pits under the buses. Heroic attempts were made to get out these unfortunate busmen. In this the commander of stretcher depot eight played a part that deserves to be recorded. Other men had been blown under buses and were unconscious. He rescued three of them and returned four times. His attempts to get the two men out of the pits were in vain. The garage was completely destroyed and with it 65 buses. Water used by the fire fighters became so hot when the flames heated the hydrants, that rescuers were scalded as they ran in to rescue the trapped.' Seven men died. Being an ex-Tilling garage, Croydon had a large collection of elderly, petrol-engined buses which, the tanks full ready for next day, simply exploded.

This was the last really ferocious raid carried out by the Luftwaffe, whose attentions would in a few weeks' time be directed towards the Russian front. The RAF steadily gained control over the skies of Southern England and the Channel until by D-Day piloted German aircraft hardly dared venture aloft, but the defences would still have to deal with the menace of the later V1 flying bombs and V2 rockets.

14

Life goes on

Thankfully Hitler, when the chips were down, proved to be a very flawed strategist, refusing to listen either to the advice of his generals or that of the ghost of Napoleon. The attack on Russia, which began at dawn on 22 June 1941, codenamed Operation 'Barbarossa', was initially highly successful and brought the German forces to the gates of Moscow and Leningrad. But a combination of the seemingly inexhaustible reserves of Russian soldiers, which Stalin was quite prepared to sacrifice in order to stem the enemy advance, and the old adversary, the fearsome Russian winter, proved insuperable. It also meant a long breathing space for London, the Luftwaffe turning its attention eastwards. Daylight raids became almost a thing of the past; we would be sent off to school by our parents, pretty secure in the knowledge that we would return home safely and, although the sound of aircraft engines still caused us to anxiously scan the skies, we could be pretty sure the aircraft was 'one of ours'.

However, there were still what were euphemistically called 'incidents', and one of the most horrific occurred in the Ilford High Road in March 1943. ST657 was a standard ex-LGOC 48-seat example of the class, delivered early in 1931 and working from Seven Kings (AP) garage. During the morning rush hour on Friday, 12 March it was heading down Ilford High Road on the 86A Limehouse to Upminster route, in the charge of Henry Brown, an Ilford man who had been driving buses for 20 years. In an interview in the *Ilford Recorder* of 18 March a passenger on the bus, Mrs M. R. Rodwell, told what happened next.

'I was in a bus that was crowded with war workers. Luckily all of them except my neighbour, who is a war worker, got out at the previous stopping place. The bus started and it had not gone many yards when it came to a sudden halt, which put a jar through me. A sudden swish of 'planes and machine guns filled the air, and we threw ourselves on the bottom of the bus, hoping to evade the oncoming bullets, but as they struck the bus they rolled down and bounced off my coat.

In order to conserve fuel, once the morning rush hour was over, a number of buses were parked in Central London to await their evening call-up rather than returning to their garages. A group is seen here in Lambeth Palace Road in 1941. *Pamlin Prints / Author's collection*

85

'As I quickly ducked again my hair caught alight from the flames that were spreading over the bus. Our knees were cut and bruised from the falling glass, and we helped each other out, saying, "God, we're bombed." At the time I was so shocked I forgot completely about the driver and conductor, the only thing my neighbour and I were thinking about was getting out ourselves. I know it seems funny but it was so sudden. We clambered out of the bus which by this time was burning rapidly, and started to run across the road and in doing so I saw another 'plane coming.

'He deliberately came our way and dropped a bomb. I am certain he was after the bus again as the flames were red and the bus must have been outstanding as it was the only vehicle in the road. As we continued across the road he swished over and things were as clear as daylight, his guns still blazing, and I could imagine the sneer on their faces as they did this indiscriminate thing. When we got to the other side of the road we asked for a drink of water. Our faces were black, our hair was singed and our legs very painful, but we said to each other we are alive. I went straight to work.' The report adds that Mrs Rodwell has four sons in the forces and when she arrived at work she said: 'Sorry I am dirty, I had a slight delay.'

Elsewhere in the paper is an account of the fate of the driver. 'A bus conductor, Mr McLaughlin, who lived almost opposite the scene and was off duty, told a reporter how he watched the petrol bus burn and a colleague, Driver Brown, trapped in his driving cab, burnt to death. He said, "There was a terrific explosion, and the bus immediately burst into flames. The driver was trapped in his seat and could not get out. There was no hope for him: we could not get near him".' A week later the *Ilford Recorder* gave a lengthy account of the driver's funeral which was attended by his widow, his 13-year-old daughter, 'the Superintendent of Seven Kings Garage ... several inspectors and a large attendance of drivers and conductors, numbering over 120'.

Houses, schools, shops and churches were all destroyed or damaged in the raid. An LPTB inspector, Mr King, was killed in a trolleybus, probably a 693, which shared the Ilford High Road with the 86A bus route. The conductor of the trolley said: 'The plane swept low over the top of the road, blasting away with its machine guns and cannon shells. One of those shells swept nearly all the seats off the top deck of the trolleybus and killed the inspector as he sat, the only passenger on the upper deck.'

One of the most remarkable escapes was that of the butchery manager of the local Co-op, a Mr Kneller, who dashed into the shop's refrigerator, dragging a boy, the only other occupant of the shop, in with him. He described what happened next. 'We hadn't been in there a few seconds when we were blown on our faces by the force of an explosion outside. We were in there some little time when I thought it was time we got out. I said to the lad: "We had better hop it!"

'We did, but I don't know how we did it. There, an amazing sight met me. The whole place was blazing and the meat was cooking like a Sunday dinner. Somehow we got through to the street.'

Mr Kneller had served in World War 1 and had survived Gallipoli. 'They used to shell us 6am to 6pm. "Trade unionists" they were, but there was no trade-unionism about this.'

A train-load of Sherman tanks at Acton Underground works in 1943. *Author's collection*

Above: Three London Transport draughtsmen photographed on 20 October 1943, with the winter tram and trolleybus schedules which they had 'been working on from three to four months at seven days a week to complete the 900 new timetables and the hundreds of duty schedules … which will increase the speed and prevent the crawling of buses'.
Ian Allan Library

Above: 'Seeing It Through' — an Eric Kennington poster, featuring a female member of Underground staff, commissioned by London Transport in 1944.
London Transport Museum

Above: 'HR2' tram No 2000 at the Abbey Wood terminus of route 38. Although this picture was taken after the war, the horse contentedly munching from his nosebag whilst having a rest from delivering milk is a reminder of the many thousands of horses still at work in London in the 1940s.
Author's collection

15

The fleet: augmentation and depredation

In late September 1940, at the height of the Blitz, LPTB Chairman Lord Ashfield had appealed for help to cover the losses to enemy bombing. In fact these losses were not that great, being no more than around 1% of the bus fleet, and there were plenty of vehicles in store. The minutes of the LPTB Board of Directors of 7 November 1940 refer to the provision of 'alternative transport by bus to replace railway, tramway and trolleybus services damaged by enemy action', and goes on to record that 'the Ministry of Transport and the Regional Commissioners throughout the country have so far secured the loan of about 500 buses for use in London upon terms to be arranged'. The 475 provincial buses were a pretty mixed bunch. Inevitably AECs and Leylands were in the majority, but there were a few ADCs, otherwise long vanished from the streets of London, and a

number of complete strangers, Crossleys from, inevitably, Manchester, and Albions, from — surprise, surprise — Glasgow. All, apart from Blitz casualties, had gone home by February 1942.

Eighteen trolleybuses also arrived. These were Sunbeams from Bournemouth. They were sent to Ilford depot to work local services and so never approached Central London. Had they done so I would, no doubt, have been amazed to see these bright yellow apparitions and probably been even more amazed if I had known that during 1944/5 I would travel on one every day to and from school when they were much needed back home, not just for my educational purposes but to help convey the thousands of American servicemen stationed in and around the town and who would shortly be embarking on the D-Day invasion fleet.

A Glasgow Corporation Albion Venturer passing St Martin-in-the-Fields in 1941. *Author's collection*

On the debit side, just about all the remaining Tilling STs, some 146 vehicles, were lent to provincial operators, the first five going to Coventry in November 1941 after the fearful bombing of that city which suffered, along with many deaths of its citizens, the destruction of its cathedral. It is remarkable that the two cathedrals in the City of London or within yards of it, St Paul's and Southwark, survived. The dramatic pictures of the former, surrounded by smoke and flames but still standing, went around the world, a symbol of London's defiance in the face of Nazi attempts at annihilation. The Tillings were followed by 143 LGOC-type STs which, between July 1942 and March 1943, took themselves off to various English, Welsh and Scottish towns and cities.

ST631 on loan to Trent in 1942. *A. D. Packer*

ST512 far from home, abroad in fact, on loan to Young's of Glasgow c1942. Whilst retaining LT livery and legal lettering it also has Young's legal lettering. Note the exhortation to use Swan Vestas matches sparingly — especially during the blackout, Glasgow and its vast dock and shipbuilding area along the Clyde suffering as grievously from the attentions of the Luftwaffe as the London Docks. *Ian Allan Library*

Of course, vehicles, wherever they may be, are of no use without drivers and conductors, and to replace men who had gone off to war women had taken up a variety of jobs on the buses, trams and trolleybuses, as well as the Underground, one account noting, somewhat patronisingly, that 'some actually became

Left: "I say, do you think I shall look awfully silly in this?" An only slightly posed picture of a newly recruited conductress and the driver of Cricklewood's STL2035, taken sometime in the summer of 1940. *London Transport Museum*

Right: Women conductors were employed from the summer of 1940, initially in the Country Area. Here a smiling 'clippie' poses somewhat precariously on a forward-entrance STL. *Author's collection*

craftsmen'. Under the headline 'Women Bus Drivers Now on Double-Deckers' the 22 March 1941 edition of *Modern Transport* included a piece about Miss Agnes Prow, 'who is now licensed to drive a double-deck bus on Young's Bus Services Glasgow–Johnstone route'. Fair enough, except that the accompanying picture of Miss Prow about to climb into her cab clearly depicts an RT! This could only have been RT19, which AEC sent on a publicity drive around the UK and which spent part of November 1940 working for Young's.

However, equality of treatment of the sexes was still well into the future. An appalling example of prejudice against women in the workplace appeared in the 17 May edition of *Modern Transport* which reported that Sunderland Corporation had dismissed a bus conductress on her marriage to a merchant seaman. The department was 'sorry to lose her' but was following a ruling by the Northern Area General Managers of Transport Committee. The vice-chairman of this committee was actually opposed to this ruling and was going to ask for it to be reversed, quoting Ernest Bevin, the Minister of Labour, who 'was appealing to all women to offer themselves for national service'.

The same edition noted that 'North-country girls working in the South of England' on enquiring at Victoria Coach Station about departures to the north had been given the reply, 'Nothing, worse luck,' because United Automobile Services Ltd had been told that the daily service to Newcastle 'could not be considered an essential service' and they must withdraw it. Which was a severe blow to the Geordie girls, 'who will find railway travelling too expensive unless a special cheap rate is instituted for their benefit'.

One fairly minor modification — but one which greatly changed the appearance of London's double-deck buses — was the reduction from late 1941 of destination displays. The route number and destination spaces were blanked out, usually painted black although red was used in a few odd cases, and the remaining 'via' space showed the number, destination and, usually, two 'via' points. Because Country Area double-deckers might work several different routes during their daily stint of duty the number space remained in use. Trams and trolleybuses, which had never been anything like as generous in the route information they displayed, were largely unaffected.

Above: The caption on this London Transport official picture taken on 14 May 1943 reads: 'Practical instruction on a service bus, with an experienced woman conductor.' Although the photograph is obviously posed, the passengers, including at least two in military uniform, are (presumably) genuine. Note the masked lighting. *Ian Allan Library*

Left: The caption for this photograph, taken on the same occasion, reads: 'The right way: left hand holds rack, thumb on punch trigger. Right hand free to insert ticket.' Preservationists intent on complete authenticity, please note. *Ian Allan Library*

Left: The third picture in this sequence, although its caption, reading 'Correct way to hold ticket-rack', is chiefly of interest in that it shows tickets which had fare stages printed on them. Junior bus- and tram-spotters longed to get hold of one of these racks but never did, having to make do with vastly inferior flimsy toy ones and tin punches. *Ian Allan Library*

Below: Another official London Transport picture. The caption reads 'Girl workers renovate destination blinds.' One assumes neither lady would have objected to being described thus. *Ian Allan Library*

Come on the Services!

LEND A HAND ON THE LAND

SPEND YOUR LEAVE OR SPARE TIME HELPING FARMERS

FULL DETAILS FROM YOUR CANTEEN

Above left: 'Our Wonderful Women,' a World War 2 poster. *Author's collection*

Above: A Land Girl as featured on a 1943 poster. *Author's collection*

Left: Two London Transport employees picking cabbages on the LT farm. *Author's collection*

16

The 'unfrozens'

It was all very well elderly buses being passed around the country, from fleet to fleet, the authorities attempting to plug the gaps and predict where demand would be lesser or greater, but all the time the vehicles were falling by the wayside — sometimes literally when, with street lighting abolished and headlights reduced to a glimmer, buses ran off the road and, with much reduced maintenance and few spare parts, no bus could be relied upon to function as well as it had in prewar days. Sooner or later, and it would have to be sooner, the bus manufacturers had to be allowed to build, alongside the tanks, Halifax bombers and all the other necessities of war their factories were turning out, a limited number of new buses. In February 1941, the Ministry of War Transport had asked London Transport for the Board's

requirements during the year. Informed that these envisaged 360 new vehicles the Ministry sanctioned 35. This was not a starting bid; it was a question of take it or leave it. The Board accepted and then asked if the bodies could be constructed at Chiswick. The minutes of 28 August 1941 noted that 'a decision is awaited'. The answer was 'yes', so the Board 'resolved to approve the purchase of the 35 buses at an estimated cost of £63,000 … 20 of the vehicles should be of low-height type and 15 ordinary double-deck vehicles.' This, however, dealt only with bodies and equally necessary were the chassis upon which to place them.

Early in 1941, the Ministry of Supply gave permission for a limited number of chassis upon which work had stopped in September 1939, to be completed. Upon these, bodies of a strict, tightly controlled,

A close-up of one of the 'unfrozen' Leyland TD7s of 1941 added to the STD class, although a poor imitation both mechanically and structurally of the prewar TD4s. Presumably the gent in the trilby hat with the notebook is a government inspector checking for excessive luxury.
Ian Allan Library

spartan specification were to be mounted. This included the 35 — in the event the number was 34 — mentioned in the minute of 28 August, but we will return to these shortly.

London's first complete new wartime-specification bus arrived at Chiswick Works on 24 October 1941. The chassis was a Leyland Titan TD7, the body by Park Royal. Had circumstances been different, this would have been a welcome addition to the fleet and very much in LPTB traditions, for the 100 Leyland Titan TD4s of the STD class were splendid buses and Park Royal had built hundreds of bodies for London buses and trolleybuses in the 1930s. The new bus was added to the STD class, but STD101 represented several steps back from the standard late-1930s STDs and STLs, to say nothing of the new RT class. The roof was single-skinned, as were the sides except at the lowest part, there were only four opening side windows (although there were ventilators at the front, upstairs and down), and in the roof there was a single route-indicator at the front, although this did not matter greatly, as all buses now had restricted displays. The upper-deck rear emergency window was not a window at all but sheet metal. The seats were upholstered in brown leathercloth. STD101 was painted in traditional red and broken white with black mudguards, there was no black band around the middle and the roof was brown. Silver had long been abandoned, in order to look less conspicuous from the air, and been replaced by grey, but now this too was to be replaced.

If rather spartan, STD101 and its 10 companions were at least new and had a certain sparkle so proved quite acceptable to passengers. Sadly, when it came to performance, sparkle was noticeable by its absence and drivers hated them. Although it had the powerful 8.6-litre direct-injection Leyland engine, the wartime STD was a sluggish performer on account of flexible engine mounting, a heavy flywheel and high gearing, which made gear changing painfully slow. It has never been clear why these 11 buses spent their entire, short careers at Victoria (GM), the LPTB's most central garage, where they worked some of the most heavily patronised routes, for which they were quite unsuited. I used to see them regularly at the summit of my bike rides to Crystal Palace, the terminus of the 137 upon which they worked until withdrawal early in 1951. Perhaps surprisingly, they served as trainers for some four years after that, the theory presumably being that if you could master a wartime STD you could drive anything.

All this is rather peculiar when one considers that members of the RT class continued to be delivered, if very slowly, until February 1942, all to totally peacetime specifications, whilst the last 'P1' trolleybus took up work in September 1941, also showing no sign of wartime cutting of corners, just one month before STD101 arrived.

The spring of 1942 saw the arrival of more buses with utility Park Royal bodies, but this time they were mounted on Bristol chassis. As with the STDs they were a mere handful, just nine, nothing like the numbers London required. They signalled an ever greater break with London traditions than STD101-11 had managed. They had Gardner engines and were, in typical Bristol manner, hardly the smoothest riding buses but drivers found them far from unsatisfactory. Taller than was usual for their type, at 14ft 6in, they were sent to Hanwell garage, which not only had a front door sufficiently high to let them in, but also where the staff were familiar with the Gardner engine, which was fitted to the 'Bluebird' LTs operated by Hanwell on route 105. Late in their careers, they were fitted with AEC engines, but this did not save them from early withdrawal, although they lasted rather longer than the STDs; the original Bs ended their careers in London in February 1953.

What the LPTB desired, if not more than gold then certainly very greatly, were AECs, and its wish was granted in December 1941, when 11 new members of the STL class were delivered to High Wycombe garage, followed by 17 to Amersham, four to Watford High Street and one to Godstone between January and October 1942. These were further examples of buses whose chassis had been under construction when war broke out and were completed 'unfrozen' — a term which came to be applied to all 447 such buses supplied to operators throughout the UK. Of course, it had been planned that STL2647 should be the very last member of its class, although STL2645 was actually the last to be delivered, to Alperton garage on 4 September 1939, one day after the outbreak of war, and 338 of their successors, the RTs, were on order. Because of the war numbers only reached RT151 before production was suspended, not being resumed (and then to a somewhat modified design) until 1947.

There had been many variations of STL since the first, boxy-looking General 1STL1s appeared in January 1933, and the 'unfrozen' 17STL chassis — we'll come to the bodies in a moment — of 1941/2 were no exception. STL2648-81 (FXT 371-404) were of standard 'provincial' specification with 'crash'-type gearboxes, friction clutches and 6.5:1

differentials. Unlike the contemporary unfrozen STDs these variations meant that they were powerful vehicles, ideally suited for mountaineering and, although there were no genuine mountains within LPTB territory, the next best thing were the slopes of the Chilterns and the North Downs, and so they came to be a familiar sight zooming up Amersham Hill in Beaconsfield and between Caterham Valley and Caterham on the Hill, a number being transferred later in 1942 to Godstone garage for routes 409 and 411 which scaled these latter heights on their way from Forest Row and Reigate to West Croydon. Forest Row was well into Sussex, set on the slopes of the Ashdown Forest, which will for ever be associated with Winnie the Pooh and his friends, their creator, A. A. Milne, living in a forest village. I got to know the 'unfrozens' well, but always opted for a forward-entrance STL if I had the choice,

simply because a forward-entrance double-decker was such a rare phenomenon.

Now to the rest of the STL-class Chiswick-built bodies of 1941. These were allocated the STL17 body code but, unlike the chassis, were totally of wartime construction, Chiswick beginning work on them in the summer of 1941. Although there were initially only 12 of them, wartime conditions meant that they were not completed until January 1942. Why only 12, you may ask, when there were 34 chassis? The answer is that the first bodies were completed before the first chassis arrived and they were therefore mounted on newly overhauled existing chassis. Externally the STL17 bodies looked much like the 1939-vintage STL16 roofbox variety, even down to the longer radiator, although this latter was painted black all over. However, shortage of glass meant that many windows were boarded over, although there was a far more generous allocation of opening windows than the unfrozen STDs could sport, whilst internally there were a number of differences. Seats reverted to the older, wooden-framed variety, polished aluminium being a scarce commodity in wartime reserved for aircraft manufacture, although they were covered in RT-style moquette, a timelessly classic design. The colour scheme was basically all-

B24, one of the second batch of austerity Bristols supplied to London Transport, at the Wembley terminus of the 92. Fitted with AEC engines, these buses were quite well regarded at Hanwell (HW) garage, where they were based, and although their bodies were no more substantial than those of other 'wartime' buses they soon found new owners when sold and, rebodied, served them longer than they had London Transport. *The Omnibus Society*

brown up to just below the ceiling, and the lower panels were not lined. The last three STL17 bodies were actually mounted on unfrozen chassis.

They were followed by yet another variation, the STL17/1, which suffered rather more from wartime restrictions, having no roof number box and no usable rear display at all. A most interesting variation, already referred to, then followed, which despite the war could be said to comply with Chiswick's standards in a manner which not even the RT class could achieve. These were the 20 low-height bodies, the STL19. Although internally they were pretty spartan, externally they were pure Chiswick, a well proportioned variation on the STL theme. The STL17/1 bodies were, with one exception, all mounted on unfrozen chassis and put to work in the Country Area, but all the lowbridge STL19 bodies were fitted to existing, standard chassis. They worked on both Central and Country Area routes. Three which worked the 462 out of Addlestone garage and served several Vickers works in the area were painted grey in order to be as inconspicuous as possible, whilst eight others came out in brown.

The pigment used in Chiswick red was in short supply and whilst an alternative was available this was likely to turn pink within a fairly short time.

The notion of the streets of London and its suburbs being served by bright pink buses, trams and trolleybuses was just too, too upsetting, my dear. As any user of plasticine will know, the more colours you add to a mix the more brown it will become, and thus this was the easiest colour to obtain in wartime. Lord Ashfield, no less, having inspected STL1776 at Chiswick in September 1940 decked out in what was officially red oxide, but like all fancy names allocated to colours hid the truth, which was a fairly bright shade of brown, gave it his approval and this became, if not the standard LT livery, then one which many buses and a few trams and trolleybuses received until red once more became obtainable towards the end of the war, although it took several years for the brown to disappear.

The last of the wartime STLs was lowbridge STL2311. Entering service in June 1943, it would prove to be the last normal-production bus ever turned out at Chiswick, which henceforward concentrated on overhauls.

STL2229, with one of the wartime lowbridge bodies mounted on a prewar chassis, stands ahead of a 9T9 at Woking in postwar days. *Author's collection*

Right: STL2679, one of the 'unfrozen' STLs which was fitted with an original LGOC 60-seat body and painted green. It is seen here postwar in use as a staff bus based at Hounslow and carrying trade plates. The body appears to be in very much better condition than most buses of its age with no sign of sagging. The group of young, impecunious enthusiasts very nearly raised enough money to preserve it; they were to succeed with other ventures. *Author's collection*

Below: STL2680, the penultimate 'unfrozen' example of 1942 working from Godstone garage. The body, whilst clearly belonging to the STL family, lacks a number indicator, has non-opening windows at the front of the upper deck and internally is distinctly spartan. It has the long radiator as fitted to the final, 1939-vintage standard STLs, but without any brightwork. *Michael Rooum*

17

The Utilities

The 'unfrozen' buses, although better than nothing, were so few in number that they did very little to satisfy the ever growing need for replacement vehicles, and so in 1942 the Ministry of War Transport authorised Guy Motors of Wolverhampton to start the manufacture of double-deck chassis, whilst various firms, including Park Royal, Weymann, Duple, Massey and Northern Counties were allowed to build the bodies. It had been hoped that Leyland could also restart production, but in the event it was so committed to tank engines (the power units for military tanks, not *Thomas*-type 0-6-0Ts) that it had to back out, leaving the field solely, initially, to Guy. This did not go down well at Chiswick which had had nothing to do with the make since getting rid of various examples passed to it by pre-1933 independents; indeed no Guy double-deckers had been built since 1936, but anything was possible, as well as an awful lot which was impossible in wartime, and so London Transport would eventually, by April 1946, find itself the owner, although not exactly a proud one, of 435 Guy Arabs.

We have already seen that a very strict, basic specification was devised for bodies and although the various builders took heed of this there were a surprising number of variations on the theme. Park Royal and Weymann were two providers of bodies for the Arabs with which London Transport was perfectly familiar but it also had to take examples from Duple, Massey, Northern Counties and Northern Coachbuilders. Duple, being based at Hendon, was hardly a stranger but was best known for high-quality coach bodies, whilst the products of the other three were largely confined 'Up North', where they were based.

Guy Arab G1, fitted with a Park Royal body, was delivered to Chiswick in late August 1942 but it took some while for its companions to arrive, so that it was not until December of that year that they began work, from Tottenham garage, on route 76. They replaced, gradually, STs and LTs which found work elsewhere. Although numerous enough to become very familiar in some parts of London Transport territory none was ever sent to garages south of the Thames and, indeed, only regularly appeared on that side of the river, certainly latterly, on the short section of the 76 between Westminster and Blackfriars Bridges. Once delivery of the 37 vehicles needed at Tottenham garage was well under way, they then began to appear at Hanwell garage and the fairly close-by Alperton; Hanwell and Alperton shared route 83A. At Hanwell they met — and were compared unfavourably with — the B class. Eventually the north-east and east proved to be the happiest stamping grounds of the Guys, for in addition to those at Tottenham they could be found working out of Enfield, Barking, Upton Park and Hornchurch garages. The G class were very much suburban buses, the 76 and the 23, which ran from Marylebone to Becontree Heath, being the only routes on which they regularly appeared which served the City and the West End. I can recall only once travelling in a G, on the 76 from Victoria, and in my downstairs seat I had to stretch to get much of a view out. I was more impressed by a ride on another route which terminated at Victoria, the 38. This was worked by LTs with open staircases. I lingered on this unique vantage point for as long as I could as we headed up towards Hyde Park Corner before being hauled inside by my mother.

In service the Arab proved something of a curate's egg, but it could have been a lot worse, given that it was a more or less untried design. The Gardner 5LW engine, with which the great majority were fitted, was not really powerful enough — a few had the more powerful 6LW — which was why the Guys were allocated to routes which encountered few hills and why so many lived in Essex, where before ascending to the upper deck of a double-deck bus it has been known for residents to ask the conductor where the

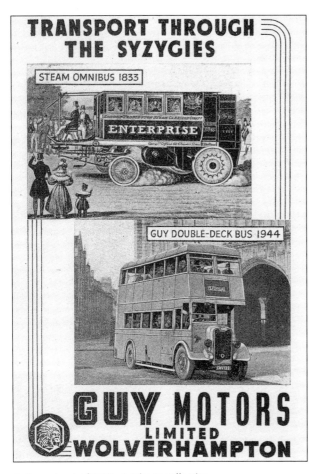

TRANSPORT THROUGH THE SYZYGIES

STEAM OMNIBUS 1833

ENTERPRISE

GUY DOUBLE-DECK BUS 1944

GUY MOTORS LIMITED WOLVERHAMPTON

A Guy advert of 1944. *Author's collection*

oxygen masks are stored. The brakes, thank goodness, were reliable and the steering satisfactory, whilst passengers found the ride pretty smooth. A number of teething troubles soon manifested themselves but these were eventually ironed out with the ready help of Guy Motors. In fact many operators found the Guy Arab a pretty good, robust bus to the extent they ordered it in considerable numbers once peacetime conditions returned, Southdown and East Kent being examples which immediately spring to mind. Even London Transport bought an Arab III, G436, in 1950 with the idea that a modified Arab chassis might be fitted with the standard RT body; nothing came of this.

Bodies were a different matter. As we have seen they were of a pretty basic nature but worse was the use of unseasoned timber, whilst corrosion added to the problems. Shortages of all sorts of materials plagued manufacturers at the height of the war and in 1943 wooden-slatted seats became the norm for a

while. If this sounds very basic it was, but as readers will know modern mainland European city transit systems, particularly trams and Underground trains, often have seats which are without cushions and are perfectly acceptable on a short ride. It all depends on the suspension. Twenty-first-century systems are vastly superior to those of 60-70 years ago, but the wartime Arabs were not bad in this respect and few passengers, well used to putting up with all sorts of wartime inconveniences and worse, complained. Possibly the ugliest feature of the utility bodies was the lack of curves, particularly on the rear dome. A shortage of panel beaters and the complexity of creating curves meant squared-off front corners and angular 'lobster back' domes.

The body manufacturers were only too aware of how far below peacetime standards their products were and worried that operators might be reluctant to place orders with them after the war. Within the limits imposed they still managed to impart a certain individuality to their designs, particularly to later batches which came out as the war was ending or immediately afterwards. Perhaps the most distinctive were those of Northern Counties, of Wigan, which fitted bodies to 102 Guys. The firm had adopted metal-framed construction in the 1930s and so was allowed to continue with this during the war. Northern Counties' first Guy body arrived just as the war in Europe was ending, in May 1945, and the company quickly moved away from full austerity restrictions, fitting a full complement of opening windows, radiused window-pans and plenty of external curves. However, the first 22 had wooden seats, and were painted brown. Indeed, they retained this colour until being repainted in the summer of 1948, whilst the last Guy to have wooden seats, G168, kept them until February 1949. Because of their much better condition, the Northern Counties Guys had no trouble finding purchasers when London Transport retired them in 1951/2.

The only wartime Guy which has survived into preservation with its utility body is G351, which is of Park Royal manufacture — which is probably fitting as this is just about the most typical looking of the wartime designs. Sold to Burton-upon-Trent in 1953, it was reconditioned, but looked very little different, and worked until early 1967. It was then bought by that renowned preservationist, John, now the Reverend John, Lines who sold his life insurance to do so, and it has only recently been completely restored by the London Bus Preservation Trust at Cobham so, whilst it looks just as it did when it first entered service from Upton Park garage in February 1946, it is now in probably the soundest condition it has ever experienced.

Guy could not produce as many double-deck chassis as were needed. Bedford had been building its little 32-seat, normal-control OWB single-decker since 1942, but this was of no use to London Transport (although in 2008 *Classic Bus* magazine produced an amusing spoof, asserting that in fact it had bought a small batch and featuring some delightful coloured illustrations of the liveries they might have worn). The real answer lay with Daimler for although its main factory and most of the contents had been destroyed in the Blitz on Coventry in November 1940, the company had other factories, including one almost next door to Guy at Wolverhampton. Daimlers said it could produce a wartime version of its established prewar COG5 chassis and the first six for London Transport, CWA6s ('W' standing for wartime, whilst 'A6' denoted a six-cylinder AEC engine — right up LT's street), arrived in April and May 1944.

The bodywork of Nos D1-6, built by Duple, was unusual by London Transport standards, like 20 of the STL bodies of 1942/3 being of lowbridge layout — although there the resemblance ended. If one lived in many parts of the UK, particularly within the Tilling empire, buses with peculiar upper-deck layouts with four-a-side seats and a side gangway, which latter feature walloped those sitting downstairs on the offside

Not a pretty sight. D1 as delivered to Merton garage in May 1944. The registration is painted directly onto the panelling, there are no rear or side route indicators, and curves are kept to a minimum, especially on the roof.
London Transport Museum

seats if they jumped up on preparing to alight without due care and consideration, were the norm. During our stay in Bournemouth in 1944/5 I travelled regularly on such vehicles and much enjoyed the novelty, but then being a fairly standard-sized seven-year-old my head was in no danger of contacting the ceiling if I should happen to be sitting downstairs. Which I almost never was, for what's the point of travelling by double-decker if you can't sit upstairs? I was also up to scratch agility-wise and could manoeuvre myself past three adults upstairs without treading on too many feet. Finally, my height ensured I could also see out of the windows. But with adults, lowbridge buses were not flavour of the month, and all the disadvantages of ECW-bodied Hants & Dorset Titans applied equally to London's lowbridge Duple-bodied Daimlers. I was reminded forcibly of this whilst taking a breather from working on this chapter to ride on the upper deck of a preserved RLH between Slough and Windsor and, given the rather more ample proportions of many present-day middle-aged or elderly gentlemen compared with 60 years ago, four to an upper-deck seat would today be a physical impossibility.

Seen in 1946 in Regent Street, ahead of an STL on route 60, is a wartime Daimler from Merton garage on route 88. This was one of the few routes regularly worked into the heart of London by wartime buses. *Author's collection*

The lowbridge Ds seated 55 passengers — only one fewer than that of a standard STL and some 20 more than a single-decker — and so were of great value during the war and for some time afterwards. What made the London lowbridge Daimlers even less acceptable was the fitting of wooden seats. Cornering on a lowbridge bus entailed upstairs passengers' holding on pretty tight, especially if one was seated next to the gangway, and wooden seats only added to the fun. Mind you, cornering Marble Arch in a Green Line RF, which I did regularly at one time, replicated this hazard quite effectively.

The lowbridge Ds were sent to Merton garage to work the 127, a virtually circular route. It had originally been single-deck route 245, but the extra demand placed on it in wartime meant that single-deckers were now inadequate. A low bridge at Worcester Park ruled out ordinary double-deckers, but by a stroke of luck several of the Crossleys and Titans lent to London in 1941 were of lowbridge layout, so the route became 127, and these migrants from 'Up North' inaugurated it. They soon returned whence they had come, to be replaced by some lowbridge STs drafted in from the Country Area, later augmented by lowbridge STLs. With the delivery of four more lowbridge Daimlers in November 1945 the Ds established an almost complete monopoly, although the STs and STLs

D8 of Merton garage on a short working of Central London route 88 from Mitcham to Acton Green, as delivered in the summer of 1944. It has wartime markings and its Duple body has only one opening window each side on each deck, all the windows being covered with protective mesh.
John Lines collection

sometimes occasionally reappeared. The Ds would eventually be replaced in 1952 by RLH-class lowbridge AEC Regents, and the route itself was destined to disappear following the disastrous six-week strike of 1958.

Although no lowbridge D has survived, a rather cunning version of one is in the fleet of Quantock Motor Services, that enterprising Somerset operator. This is CCX 777, a Duple-bodied CWA6 delivered to Huddersfield Corporation in July 1945. Although not absolutely identical to the London Ds —the windows, for example, having sliding vents instead of half-drops, and the indicators being different — when CCX 777 reappeared in 2008 repainted in London all-red livery and numbered D130 on route 127 it caused something of a sensation and, viewed from the right angle, looked remarkably like the real thing.

The rest of the Daimlers delivered to London Transport between April 1944 and November 1946 were of normal highbridge layout. Their bodies were identical to those fitted to the austerity Leylands, Bristols and Guys, the great majority being built by Duple. Thirty-seven of these wore a livery strikingly different from that seen on any other 'wartime' bus — they didn't enter service until early 1946 — being

painted green for working the 721/722 routes between Aldgate and Brentwood and Upminster. Green Line services were coming back on stream and these heavily patronised routes had always needed double-deckers, STLs having previously been used. It hardly needs to be said that austerity-bodied Daimlers did not enhance the Green Line image, although in truth Green Line was always rather more of an express bus operation than true coach work, as Southdown, or Royal Blue for example understood it. Some of the Daimlers were painted green and cream, some the traditional two shades of green, with the Green Line roundel between decks, and they certainly looked attractive. These aside, all D-class buses were sent to Merton — and even the Green Line vehicles would end up there.

There was one other group of vehicles which arrived in wartime. These were 43 trolleybuses. They diverged as greatly from the London norm as did any of the austerity motor buses, although they were certainly much better appointed. Despite the delivery of the final 'prewar'-design trolleybuses, the 'P1s', in April 1941, London Transport had told the Ministry of War Transport that more were needed to compensate for damage by enemy action and the solution was a pretty surprising if logical one. Twenty-five MCW-bodied Leylands had been ordered by Durban, South Africa, but could not be sent out owing to war conditions. Why leave them idle when London was in need? Of squarish aspect, 8ft wide and with various features needed to cope with the heat of the South African city, they needed several modifications carried out at Fulwell. This done, they were classified 'SA1' and 'SA2', numbered 1722-46 and sent to work at Ilford, where they were employed on local routes. They were joined by 18 AECs intended for Johannesburg, again with MCW bodywork; these were classified 'SA3'. All were at work by the beginning of June 1943, remaining at Ilford until withdrawn in the mid- and late 1950s.

An MCW advertisement featuring No 1764, one of the trolleybuses intended for South Africa but diverted to London Transport and used in the Ilford area.
Ian Allan Library

18

A new terror from the skies

The first flying bomb descended on London seven days after D-Day, around dawn at 4.21am on 13 June 1944, hitting a bridge spanning some LNER tracks near Stratford. London Transport's first encounter was on 29 June, when Bexleyheath depot was hit and 38 trolleybuses destroyed or severely damaged. Flying bombs, or V1s, were fired from mobile launch sites in Northern France, Belgium and the Netherlands and the advancing Allied troops were constantly forcing them to move on. Nevertheless they wrought terrible damage and did nothing for civilian morale, for they were as likely to arrive during the day as at night. And this at a time when raids by manned aircraft had almost ceased, for the RAF and the USAAF had virtually driven the Luftwaffe from the skies over the English Channel.

There were three methods of bringing a V1 down before it reached London. The anti-aircraft guns were concentrated on two areas, along the coast between Dover and Beachy Head and in a box-like area around the Thames and Medway estuaries. Then some 1,600 barrage balloons barred the missiles' way. Finally there was RAF Fighter Command, which operated clear of the area given over to the anti-aircraft guns. By this date there were Typhoons, successors of the Hurricanes, and advanced marks of the Spitfire, both of which could exceed 400mph and could match the speed of the missiles. The principal RAF aerodrome in the fight against the V1s was West Malling, up on the downs above Maidstone, where your author served during National Service some 13 years later, strategically placed between the coast, the Medway, and London. If possible the fighters met the V1s way out over the English Channel and brought them down crashing harmlessly into the sea. The most effective way for a fighter to bring down a V1 was either to fire at it from a distance or fly close to it so that the airflow disturbed its balance and it crashed to earth. This, clearly, had to be done away from built-up areas and was not without risk to pilots. There was an instance of a pilot who realised that a

A V1 flying bomb over South East London in September 1944.
Author's collection

disabled V1 was about to crash on Bethesda Hospital in Margate, and fired at close range, so that it disintegrated but the wreckage hit his Spitfire and caused his death. Something like 8,500 V1s were launched at Southern England and all but 2,500 were brought down before they could reach London.

The earlier types of flying bomb dived straight into the ground, this absorbing much of the force of the explosion, but in later examples the engine would cut out, and the V1 would glide to earth. This gave those on the ground some 15 seconds to react, which was often enough to gain some sort of cover, but when it landed the blast would be much greater. One of the most horrific incidents took place in the Aldwych.

I can recall only too clearly the drone of a V1 — we called them 'doodlebugs' or 'buzz-bombs', nicknames which somehow gave the illusion of humanising them — and, much worse, the sudden silence, as the engine, which sounded not unlike a very noisy motor cycle, stopped and you waited for it to fall out of the sky. We had been making our annual visit to Shropshire in June 1944 and we arrived home from Paddington station by, as usual, 36 bus to Victoria, Southern Electric to Norbury, and a 16 or 18 tram from there to the Pond. Although that June was, weather-wise, not up to much this day was bright and sunny, the sort of weather which typifies what a June evening should be. Mum had just got the tea ready, Dad had arrived home from work on his bicycle, and the four (Granny made up the fourth) of us were about to sit down when there was just about the loudest bang I had ever heard. As we dashed for the Morrison shelter in the next room I looked up fully expecting to see the ceiling come down on us or at least the plaster to give way, exposing the lathes, which I had seen so often in bombed houses. We sat in silence, holding our breaths, the house remained intact and we emerged unscathed. Not so the unfortunate employees of one of the many factories off Purley Way, about a mile away. The V1 had hit the factory in Aurelia Road just as work was ending and dozens were killed.

Just around the corner from Aurelia Road was Lavender Road, where my friend Derek Riches lived. His father was a fireman with the Auxiliary Fire Service, a volunteer force which later became part of the National Fire Service. They operated grey-painted Austin fire engines, which looked a bit like delivery vans with a ladder on top. We considered them nothing like as glamorous as the regular red appliances in which the firemen sat on the outside, on full view as they dashed along, bells ringing. In reality, the AFS performed valiant work at the height of the Blitz, not only tackling

fires, but also rescuing countless numbers of air-raid victims. Derek and I used to have drawing competitions and when the dropping of the atomic bomb on Hiroshima was announced we imagined it must have been the largest bomb any aircraft could carry; it seemed inconceivable when the picture of the bomb appeared in the *Daily Mail* that something so relatively small could have caused 140,000 deaths.

Aurelia Road was the home of the old former South Met tram depot. It had ceased to be used in 1933 and the track, leading into the main Mitcham Road where the 630 trolleybuses now ran, had been disconnected, but it had been reconnected in 1936 so that withdrawn trams could be stored there and eventually broken up. A year later its roof was declared unsafe and it closed again in November 1937. I can, however, remember seeing the tracks still there and the building remained.

During the war it served a grim purpose. David Golfman was a member of the Building Volunteers who was sent in the summer of 1944 from his home in Fife to help in Croydon during the V1 and V2 attacks. He described his arrival on 6 June at his Nissen hut billet in Aurelia Road. 'It was situated on a quadrangular compound, flanked on three sides by domestic two-storey buildings and on the other by a large, brick-built tram depot.' During a raid he decided the depot will offer more protection than a Nissen hut; 'It was then I discovered it was in use as a mortuary.' He later moved to other accommodation a short distance away close to Mitcham Cemetery. After a raid he returned to his original Nissen hut beside the tram depot to find it destroyed and the occupants dead. After doing what he could for the dead and injured he helped lay out the bodies 'in the remains of the mortuary,' and was then given a warrant to go home. At King's Cross he saw to his amazement black grapes on sale and was told, 'rather haughtily' that they would cost him five shillings, 'a lot of money in those days.' He bought them and the next morning, around 7.30, handed them 'to a very surprised wife when she was still in bed alongside my small son and baby daughter.' He had had nothing to eat 'since supper two days earlier but clean or dirty I was home.'

Part of nearby Mitcham Common was used to dump thousands of tons of rubble from bombed buildings, the higher level of the ground still being obvious today. Close by is the cemetery where many victims of the bombings were buried, some in mass graves. More than 750 Croydon citizens died in air raids. Croydon and the south-east London suburbs were particularly affected, being in a direct line between the launch sites of the V1s and V2s and Central

London. It had long been known that German scientists were working on guided, pilotless weapons and bombing by the RAF and the USAAF delayed their inauguration for some six months. A story emerged after the war that the guidance systems were aimed at the centre of London, but that either a member of the Resistance or a British agent had managed to penetrate German security and modify the aiming mechanism, so that most of the V1s fell short of the City and the West End. Certainly the Croydon area suffered considerably, particularly the north end of the borough. Addiscombe received 80 hits from flying bombs and V2s, 84 people dying in the raids.

Not that Central London escaped. A terrible incident was that at the Aldwych on 30 June. In clear skies, watchers saw a V1 cut out over Waterloo station and glide down. It landed at 2.07pm between Bush House and Adastral House. Many of the surrounding buildings were steel-framed and although their stone façades crumbled and, horrifically, their windows shattered, they remained standing but the blast wrought terrible havoc inside them and especially in the streets. Inevitably, a number of buses were involved. Some of their passengers had made for shelters, other remained in the vehicles. The death toll has never been accurately calculated. Officially it was around 50, with many more injured, but because so many of the victims were Government workers it is generally believed that the real total of the dead might well have been in excess of 200.

A similar incident took place at Lewisham Market on 28 July, when the blast extended for some 600 yards in both directions. Buses and trams and their passengers were caught, and the death toll amounted to 59, which was the highest number in a V1 attack on South London.

Nothing could be done to bring down a V2, for it flew at 3,000mph. One of the designers, Wernher von Braun, was snatched up by the USA at the end of the war and led the team which eventually landed a man on the moon. Many assumed that D-Day would bring the raids to an end, indeed a Government minister said as much, but by 30 June some 70 to 100 V1s were being launched at London each day. There was near-panic amongst the public, and once again a large-scale evacuation from parts of the capital and suburbs took place. It was almost a re-run of the evacuation of September 1939. Some 2,435 extra main-line trains were organised, getting on for 400 feeder trains to connect with them were run by the Underground in addition to London Transport providing around 5,000 buses, 300 trams and 500 trolleybuses — more precise figures have been quoted but are difficult to verify. In the opposite direction, 65,800 Anderson and Morrison shelters were brought into London. There were 149 recorded incidents in which damage was caused by V1s to London Transport vehicles or property. As many as

Houses in Croydon destroyed by a V1. *Author's collection*

15,000 people were leaving from the main-line stations each day in July, and it is calculated that between 1.5 and 2 million people had gone by early September. We were among them.

This sudden exodus was noticed in all sorts of walks of life. Borrowing of books from Croydon public library was '15,351 fewer than the issues for the same period of last year'. Magistrates were now authorised to 'impose sentences up to one year for looting from premises damaged in air raids'. Previously the maximum sentence was three months. We may also note, *à propos* very little, that the previous Friday, the 13th, had been particularly unlucky, more than over 30 road accidents being reported. These included a collision between a motor car and a bus, which resulted in Mr R. W. Fox (36) receiving a compound fracture of the left leg, and a collision between bus and tramcar in North End, Croydon, the result of which was that Joseph McMillian (56), of Biggen Avenue, Mitcham, suffered a cut finger and shock.

We had said prayers in my school in Thornton Heath on 6 June for the success of the D-Day landings and for the lives of those involved. Eleven days later the first V1 fell in the Croydon area and on 1 July one fell on the houses immediately behind ours in Whitehall Road, close to the back of Thornton Heath tram depot. Five people in the houses were killed, eight houses were destroyed and 30 others, including ours, had their windows and much of their roofs blown off, rendering them uninhabitable. The tram depot suffered some blast damage. We were unharmed and moved in with relations. On 16 July during a raid on Brigstock Road, served by the 42 tram which diverged from the main 16/18 route at Thornton Heath Pond, four people were killed, the fire station damaged, and my grandmother, visiting friends nearby, was cut by flying glass, although not badly.

My father got a posting within the NAAFI organisation in which he worked to Bournemouth, and we headed off to Waterloo. There we joined thousands of others and waited. As our train pulled in, I particularly noticed a carriage with unusual vertical planking. I assumed that this was some wartime temporary repair. In fact, it would have been one of the South Eastern & Chatham Railway boat train vehicles dating from the early 1920s, not normally seen on the Waterloo–Bournemouth line, but, of course, anything was possible in wartime. We had no chance of getting a seat; instead we stood or sat on the luggage in the guard's van. It reeked of fish, and the journey seemed to take for ever.

Eventually we arrived at Southampton where enough passengers got out for us to find somewhere proper to sit. Dad had rented us accommodation over a grocer's shop in St Michael's Road, Bournemouth, close to the town centre and within walking distance of the West Cliff, where NAAFI had taken over the Beacon Hotel. I travelled each day by number 25 trolleybus — more than likely riding on one which had been lent to Ilford depot — to Westbourne Preparatory School, where the front door was in Hampshire, the back in Dorset, and the headmaster bore a passing resemblance Michael Aldridge's character, Seymour, in *Last of the Summer Wine*. Granny went to live with Uncle Will Foster at his shoe shop in Poole High Street. We used to visit her by Hants & Dorset lowbridge double-decker each Wednesday. When not investigating the mysteries of shoe repair and being shown by Uncle Will how to buff up an old penny so it gleamed as though brand new I would watch Coastal Command Sunderland flying boats taking off and landing in the harbour and see tired-looking freighters which had survived U-boat attacks being unloaded at the quayside. A tank engine regularly puffed up and down, which added to the fun but you had to be careful where you went;

Children playing on a bombsite. *Author's collection*

more than once Dad, who was always fascinated by boats and ships, and I were shooed away by sentries, when we attempted to venture into what we hadn't realised were restricted areas.

Croydon was certainly best avoided in the last six months of 1944, for it suffered more V1 attacks, 141, and a greater percentage of deaths in relation to attacks, than any other borough or area in London and the suburbs. There were, however, only four V2s which fell on Croydon. The worst incident involving London Transport staff and property took place a few hundred yards beyond the borough boundaries, at Elmers End on 18 July 1944. A V1 exploded at 8.37 in the evening in the entrance of the bus garage and the resultant blaze set alight the petrol tanks of the buses, almost entirely LTs. Seventeen people died, one a woman passer-by, two members of the Home Guard involved in rescue work and the rest London Transport employees. Amongst them was 17-year-old Sydney Steer. A few days later his father was one of 44 killed one lunchtime when a restaurant just up the road in Beckenham received a direct hit.

The aiming of the V2s seems to have been rather imprecise, for only two fell on the City of Westminster and none at all on the City of London. This compared with Ilford, which suffered 35 V2 attacks, and Woolwich, which had 33. However, if the V2 was simply a weapon of terror rather than one aimed at specific strategic targets then one has to admit it succeeded, at least in the short term. Most of the launch sites were over-run by Allied forces by the end of August 1944 and the raids tailed away, but in October V2s began to be launched and they and the V1s continued to menace London and its suburbs into 1945. The last V2 fell on the London area on 27 March 1945, the last V1 a day later. Altogether, 6,184 people were killed by V1s and V2s, and 17,981 were injured.

19

Peace at last

With the official return of the remaining evacuees in the summer of 1945, around 30 trams, 150 trolleybuses and several hundred motor buses were commandeered for one last journey, although many unofficial evacuees, such as ourselves, came back under our own steam. Well, steam as far as Waterloo, whence a 'Feltham' tram, my very favourite means of transport, brought us back to Thornton Heath: a sure and welcome sign that life was beginning to return to normal. Although getting used to peacetime was something of a novelty.

My rabbit, Nora, and the six chickens — also evacuated to a safe home (so my parents had informed me) — never did return, and our dog, Trix, having survived the Blitz, had been knocked down and killed by a farmer's car in a Shropshire lane. Cousin Joan, whose husband Fred had been killed a few days after the Normandy landings, was married again, to his brother Arthur, a sailor, and there was now a fourth second cousin, Diane. I had missed the VE Day street party but was in time for the VJ (Victory over Japan) celebration. At the same time Cousin Eric was rather nearer the centre of things, being present on his Royal Navy ship in Tokyo Bay at the surrender of the Japanese navy. He came home, resumed his work as a carpenter on the estate in Shropshire where our family had worked for generations, our great grandfather as chief groom, Great Uncle Fitz succeeding him as chauffeur to the big house, married Joyce and they are still there 62 years later.

Although I was not really aware of it at the time, London was incredibly shabby and would remain so for a decade or more, right until the 'Swinging Sixties' transformed Britain. It began with the quite wonderful 1951 Festival of Britain, served by the fast-contracting tram system as well as a series of bus routes which would be the genesis of the now enormously popular London bus tours. Our house was more or less put back together, the netting was scraped off tram, trolley, motor bus and train windows with considerable difficulty, so splendidly adhesive was the wartime glue used, and overhauls began. And were they needed! The motor bus fleet was in a dreadful state. Some 166 buses and coaches had been destroyed during the war, a relatively small number out of a fleet of some 6,400. But there had been over 4,000 instances of severe damage and an

A scene in Whitehall on VE Day, with a 'Bluebird' LT and at least two STLs swamped by the joyful crowds. *Author's collection*

almost countless number of minor scrapes. Chiswick Works and the garages had done their best mechanically, at least to the extent of keeping the buses running, even if not to prewar standards. Bodies had, perforce, been sadly neglected. Thousands of time-expired vehicles were still trundling around, windows rattling, some of them still missing glass, paintwork faded, bodies sagging, engines in need of tender loving care. The ST class, on which I mostly travelled, seemed to me to be in a particularly bad way, its members in any case some five years beyond their normal life span, their petrol engines noisy and often back-firing.

One hundred and eight members of London Transport staff had been killed whilst on duty, 48 of them tram and trolleybus staff, the rest bus or Underground; 1,867 had been injured. As for the fleet in general, many of the trams, although as neglected as the buses despite the best efforts of Charlton Works which, like Chiswick and Aldenham, was engaged on war work, were basically in better shape than the motor buses, for a tram was built more along the lines of a battleship, and stood up better to being knocked around and neglected compared with a bus, the body of which owed a great deal to pony-and-trap technology. Trolleybuses had probably survived best of all, and even when ending their careers in the early 1960s, after over 20 years' hard graft, many were by no means completely worn out. Seventeen trolleybuses were wiped out, another 61 had their bodies completely destroyed but their chassis, after repair, were fit for further use. Sixteen were rebodied by Weymann in 1941/2 and after the V1 and V2 raids of 1944/5 25 were given new, all-metal bodies by East Lancs and 20 composite bodies by Northern Coachbuilders. There was little evidence of wartime skimping in any of the rebodied vehicles, their design following pretty closely that of the later prewar 'L', 'M' and 'N' classes.

Two victory parades were held in London on 8 June 1946, one a marching column and one mechanised. My preferred choice would have been the latter but Dad decided on the former, which was no great hardship, particularly as I was provided with a periscope in case the crowds were too dense for me to see between their legs or under their armpits. This periscope was a wonderful thing which we constructed from coloured, striped cardboard and two mirrors and was supplied, so I seem to recall, free with the *Daily Mail* — my father's choice of reading matter, I hasten to add, although I had no objection to following the cartoon adventures of Teddy Tail of the *Daily Mail*,

A 1945 London Transport poster. I wonder if it could be proved that *exactly* 59,750 windows were damaged by enemy action? *London Transport Museum*

Rip Kirby, and Pop and Blondie. We took a tram to Norbury station, a train from there to Victoria and walked to Oxford Street, bus services in the centre of London having been more or less suspended. In the event, the periscope was hardly needed, as it was rather cumbersome and the crowds good-naturedly let children worm their way to the front.

The column consisted of soldiers, sailors and airmen from just about every country which had contributed to the Allied war effort. I don't recall the atmosphere was one of excessive triumphalism, more of profound relief that at last it was all over. I was old enough to be aware of the horror which was felt as the British and American troops reached and liberated the Nazi concentration camps and the revelation of what had been perpetrated there. That really did seem to come as a complete surprise to the British public, much less than finding out how the Japanese had treated their prisoners. Writing as a grandfather who has sons who have lived in both Germany and Japan, who regularly has a little Japanese girl playing in our garden with our granddaughter, and who has an Irish wife whose uncles fought for independence after eight centuries of British oppression, I am simply grateful that, whatever the shortcomings of international relations in the ensuing 60 years, the notion of England, Ireland, Germany and Japan ever again going to war is something beyond the comprehension of the 21st century.

As the last soldiers headed past us, Dad and I hurried across to Hyde Park and managed to catch a good bit of the mechanised column, including tanks and the Bren-gun carriers with which I was so familiar, but also two London buses, RT39 and RT4, a Manchester Titan and a Halifax Regent, which bore the legend 'The First Provincial Bus to Answer London's Appeal for Assistance, 22nd October 1940'. Buses, trams and trolleybuses and their crews worked overtime that day, not finishing in some cases until early next morning, ensuring that everyone got home, and a firework display taking place on the Thames opposite the Houses of Parliament at 10pm. I didn't get to see this, but a couple of evenings later marvelled at what would today be considered a very minimal lit up advertising display on the side of a building at the top of Crown Hill, Croydon. Trams, of course, passed along the top of Crown Hill every few minutes. And, as I write this, they do again. Who would have imagined that?

The mechanised Victory parade passing through Admiralty Arch on 8 June 1946. 'Prewar' RTs 4 and 39 lead Halifax AEC Regent JX 1788 and Manchester Titan VR 5755, which had helped out in London in 1940. *London Transport Museum*

Typical of the crowds which depended upon public transport
in the 1940s is this scene outside Charing Cross (nowadays
Embankment) station sometime in 1946. *London Transport
Museum*

20

Getting back to normal

Despite the fact that the war was over, raw materials remained in short supply, and new buses continued to be built to utility specification. Deliveries to London in 1946 included a final group of 100 Daimler buses, the most individual of all the austerity vehicles, in that they were much less austere, a 'halfway house' in the progression towards full peacetime specifications. The Park Royal bodies had the flat, sloping front common to all the austerity buses, very like that of a 'sit-up-and-beg' STL, but a sloping back, the lines of which were spoiled by a full peacetime, three-piece indicator which looked like a last-minute add-on designed for a quite different bus and which in the event was never fully used anyhow. They were painted in a version of what would eventually become the standard livery in the RT-family era with a cream band amidships but with an additional one dividing the upper-deck windows and the roof. All 100 were sent to Sutton garage, which meant they were a familiar sight at Morden, where many of the routes operated by Merton congregated and so Morden was very quickly dubbed 'Daimler-land' by we bus spotters. It was within cycling distance of home but I never managed to capture all 281 Ds, unlike my classmate, Hicks, who lived in Sutton. A Daimler route, the 115, passed along the A23 at the bottom of our road. It was operated jointly by Sutton and Croydon garages, the 115, so I was very familiar with the Park Royal Ds. Southdown coaches were also a familiar sight on the A23; by a coincidence the only other buses I can recall that were fitted with bodies identical to those on D182-281 were some Leyland PD1 Titans of Southdown. By *another* coincidence Croydon garage (TC) was allocated some all-Leyland PD1s in 1946 which were put into the STD class and these worked the 115 for a short while. They had engines derived from those Leyland put in wartime tanks. These, too, were identical, except for front indicators and a few minor variations, to a batch of Southdown Leylands.

STD124, a more-or-less standard provincial example of Leyland's first postwar double-deck design, the PD1, complete with Weymann body, one of 65 which arrived early in 1946. *Author's collection*

The STDs were somewhat sluggish, not as good as the prewar STDs, but vastly better than the wartime versions and found ready buyers, far away in Yugoslavia, when sold off in the mid-1950s. Likewise a final batch of 20 Bristols, AEC-engined K6As, B10-29, which joined their brothers at Hanwell at the very end of 1945 and the beginning of 1946. Although their austerity bodies soon deteriorated, there was nothing much wrong with the engines and chassis, and when London got rid of them they were snapped up by various Tilling Group companies, which had them fitted with new ECW bodies and obtained many years of useful life out of them.

Finally, there were the very last STLs. These were 20 strikingly handsome Weymann-bodied 56-seaters, the first of which arrived in late 1945, were painted green, numbered STL2682-701, and sent to Watford High Street, from where they regularly ventured to Luton on the 321 and thus encountered the only municipally owned bus fleet within London Transport's territory. I embarked upon a bus-spotting expedition to the far north in 1949, considering myself scarcely less courageous than Captain Scott — yes, I know he went south, but you know what I mean — and managed to underline a good few of them in my 'ABC'. All, being non-standard, were sold for further service. One of them, STL2692, which was sold to Grimsby Corporation in 1955 and gave it no less than 13 years' sterling service, then was bought in 1968 for preservation. It has the distinction of being the only example of all the double-deck buses of neither true austerity nor full Chiswick standard which entered service immediately after the war to survive and, restored to its original green livery, regularly graces rallies. The postwar RLH class was fitted with what was essentially a slightly updated version of the lowbridge version of this body, and several examples have been preserved.

RT97 was badly damaged by the blast from a flying bomb explosion in July 1944 and sent to Birmingham City Transport to be repaired, but this undertaking was so inundated with work that it was returned without having been attended to. The LPTB then decided to rebuild it as a pay-as-you-enter bus and it is seen in this guise in December 1945 working route 65.
Along with similarly rebuilt STL2284, the two soon proved that the system was impractical and RT97 was then repainted in Green Line livery and sent to operate from Romford garage. Here it was no more successful. It would eventually reappear in very different form as Green Line coach RTC1 in 1949.
Ian Allan Library

21

The wanderers return

The 10T10s which were taken over by the US Army and Red Cross left London Transport ownership, but were bought back in 1945/6. Twelve, however, failed to return to the fold. These were Ts 460/86/88, 509/78/86/7/94, which served as coaches for the US Army, T670/81, which were American Red Cross coaches, and T665/6, which were US 'clubmobiles'. It was assumed that all had been lost in bombings or sunk on their way to or from France but, in fact, T460 and T594 reappeared in the UK and were sold to other operators, the former to Davies of Merthyr, the latter ending up nearer home with Smith of Reading. Also acquired by the US Army were six of their 9T9 predecessors, T414/5/6/21/2/43, of which T443 failed to return.

Then there were the former Green Line 1/T7/1 coaches of 1930/1 vintage, which, although remaining in LT ownership, had been converted to staff ambulances. These were all rapidly returned to bus work, many of them as early as August 1945, and although 25 of their very slightly earlier contemporaries had been sold or converted to lorries in 1938/9, some which had been in store were brought back into service, along with the former ambulances and proved a vital addition to the hard pressed postwar fleet, some lasting into the 1950s. Others, 51 in all, were sold as the war in Europe was ending to the Control Commission, initially for service in Germany. Public transport was in a parlous state on mainland Europe, far worse than in the UK, whilst much more grave was the plight of many millions of its citizens, displaced persons who at the end of the war found themselves far from their families and homes — if these still existed. My cousin Joyce, who had worked at Bletchley Park during the war, helping decipher messages from agents in occupied Europe, in 1945 took up a post with UNRAA, the United Nations Relief and Rehabilitation organisation, and any form of transport, however elderly or alien to the part of the world in which it found itself, was a boon. The old T-class former coaches and buses might not have been in the first flush of youth, but they served Europe well for several years, helping communities to get back on their feet as life returned to normal. Amongst them was the entire batch of 5T4s, 12 Regals which were fitted with handsome Chiswick-designed Weymann bodies dating from 1935. A number of these Ts had earlier been converted to use producer gas — and then converted back again — and others had been snowplough buses. Many of these were sold to the French 'Service de Surplus', and worked in the industrial north of the country. They seem to have finally ceased work in the early 1950s, around the same time those still in London Transport ownership ended passenger duties. One, 5T4 T357, would 58 years later be repatriated from a French farm to await restoration at Cobham Bus Museum.

London Transport decided that it could also dispose of some of its 20-seat, one-man Leyland Cubs, their duties having been taken over by large-capacity vehicles, and 25 (Nos C6, 9, 10/2, 27, 33/5/7, 43/6/8, 51/4, 62/7, 71/5/9, 80/3/4/6/7/9 and 96) went to Belgium. Eight had been loaned to other UK operators during the war and, by 1948, the total was down to 68, 30 having passed into other hands; however the rear-engined version of this class, the CR, of which all had been put into store during the war, re-emerged, some serving as Central Area reliefs in 1946 and a handful taking up their intended duties in the Country Area.

The Green Line 6Q6s and the TFs had also served as ambulances. Their return to their intended activities was a protracted affair, the last seven TFs not returning until July 1948, whilst the final two Qs only re-appeared in October 1948, two years and eight months after Green Line services had started up again. Similarly the six-wheel LTC private-hire coaches had to wait until the summer of 1946 before resuming normal service. The contrast between the rapidity with which these vehicles were prepared for war service and the time scale of getting them back into civvy street emphasises the huge backlog of overhauls facing London Transport. Chiswick Works found itself almost overwhelmed. It would never again produce new bus or coach bodies (except as one-offs), and much of the extensive remedial work — in most cases amounting to a complete rebuild — required by many bodies to keep them in service for even a few more years had to be entrusted to various private firms.

Left: One of the Ts sent to Europe in 1945 pictured sometime later working in northern France. An identical 5T4, T357, was found a few years ago in a French barn and brought back to Cobham Bus Museum for restoration. *Author's collection*

Below: The Green Line is restored. Two 9T9s are seen at Chiswick on 31 January 1946. That on the right is still in wartime condition as used by American forces, that on the left, T406, has already been returned to Green Line condition, although it has been painted in green and white bus livery and its radiator painted black. *London Transport Museum*

The Tilling STs were possessed of wanderlust to a considerable degree, much of it no doubt brought about by a desire to keep out of the breakers' hands for as long as possible, as they were already past their sell-by date when the war broke out. All that were fit to run in passenger service and not destroyed by enemy action or converted for service use, that is 146 buses, were lent to provincial operators, a large number being shipped out in December 1941, many more going in January 1942, the last leaving in October 1942. A number of LGOC Central Area STs, 145 in all, also served in the provinces, as did two Country Area examples — the prototype, ST1139, which had been delivered to East Surrey in 1929, and ST1029, owned originally by Public. Presumably STs were chosen because they were of lower seating capacity than LTs and STLs and could be more easily spared.

The time spent away from London varied greatly, the shortest being that of a group which went to Hants & Dorset and Bournemouth Corporation in January 1943 and for some odd reason didn't take to life on the Hampshire coast — it cannot have been the sight of the pier with its central section removed to foil an invasion or the line of scaffolding erected at the water's edge for the same reason, for they would have witnessed far more harrowing scenes in London — and came home despite it being midsummer seven

months later. Yet two others, ex-Tilling STs 845 and 855, found the seaside so alluring that, after contrasting spells with Trent and Sheffield Corporation respectively, took up residence with Hants & Dorset and did not return to London until February 1948. These refugee STs found new homes with a wide variety of operators, varying from the mighty Midland Red, which took 23, to Paton Bros of Renfrew, which took just one, and included three which went to Hants & Sussex of Emsworth, run by the mercurial Basil Williams and thus joined a fleet inevitably known as 'Basil's Bangers'. The largest number went to Coventry Corporation, which took 28. By 1948, some 69 examples were back working in the capital, where, according to the Ian Allan 'ABC', 'they still do considerable passenger service'. In the fleet list six are marked 'to be withdrawn', which doesn't quite tally as the whole class was by then due

A wonderful collection of 'Basil's Bangers', part of Basil Williams's Hants & Sussex fleet in 1942. Flanking London Transport Tilling ST874, on loan, are, from the left, much the newest vehicle in the collection, in the form of an 'unfrozen' Leyland Titan TD7, then UF 7416, a former Southdown Short Bros-bodied TD1 Titan of 1931, two Tilling-Stevens B10A2s of 1929, the second certainly ex Southdown, a Dodge and a Morris van. Interestingly, identical examples of the ST, the Southdown TD1 and Tilling-Stevens B10A2 have survived to be preserved. *Alan Lambert collection*

for extinction as soon as sufficient RTs and RTLs had been delivered.

Mention of Basil Williams recalls an interview I once had with him, shortly before his death in his late 80s. He told me he was the only civilian to be let in on the secret of the precise date of the D-Day landings. He lived in a rather grand house in Emsworth, which is not far from Portsmouth — he used to loan it every summer to the local Conservative Party for a garden party bash until he fell out with them (or they with him, as he put it) — and during the war provided buses and coaches for a variety of military duties. One day early in 1944 he was summoned to Portsmouth and there was asked by a rear admiral if he could supply 80 vehicles sometime during May. He replied that, given fuel restrictions and the general shortage of buses, this was quite impossible. The rear admiral insisted that providing these buses was essential to winning the war. Eventually Basil prised out of him just what was afoot and was given the date of the invasion of Europe. Basil replied 'I'll see what I can do,' and did, indeed, come up trumps. He also told me that at the height of the Blitz he had put in an order for 50 new buses and coaches to be delivered immediately after the war. 'If we lose the war, what the hell? And if we win there will be such a shortage of new vehicles that if I can't use them all I'll be able to hire them out.' Which he did. Basil ran a variety of bus companies in Sussex and Hampshire and was generally a thorn in the side of Hants & Dorset, Southdown and London Transport, often being taken to court for alleged infringement of operating procedures; he just as often took one or more of his mighty adversaries to law and sometimes beat them.

In 1939 it had been London Transport's intention that by 1945 many hundreds of RTs would be in service and the tram a vanished dinosaur, replaced by the trolleybus. In the event, the war delayed all these plans. The brave new world arrived very slowly and was not all that brave, the public becoming deeply frustrated that wartime austerity seemed to be the peacetime norm, not really understanding (because they were not told) what a parlous financial state the war had left us in — deep in debt to the USA, with industries starved of investment and making do with machinery and methods out of date and a sitting target for overseas (quite often Empire) competitors. But there was full employment, the wartime coalition Government and the postwar Labour administration having determined that lessons would be learned from the failures of 1918 to create a fairer society, and two decades on, instead of facing the most horrendous war of all time, as the survivors of the Great War had done in 1939, London — 'Swinging London' — was the place to be, the cultural centre of the world, where young people, boys and girls, men and women, were more prosperous than they had ever been with greater educational, career and travel opportunities than ever before, and the red London double-deck bus was fast becoming *the* symbol of the capital.

Appendices

1: The fleet in September 1939

SINGLE-DECK BUSES

T class (AEC Regal)

106 of the original 251 Green Line coaches introduced 1930 (T51/6, 61/6, 76, 85, 94, 101/8/9/11/3/4/6/8/20/1/4/32/6/45/59, 159/60/3-5/7/9/71/2/4-6/8/80-2/4/99, 203/6-9, 211-9/23/4/6/9-37/9/40/4/8, 253/5/61-7/70-7/80/1/3/5-8/90-3/5-8, 301/2/5/6)

49 original Central Area buses, ex LGOC, introduced 1929 (T1-34/6/7/9-50, 156)

12 Central Area buses, ex Thomas Tilling, introduced 1932 (T307-18)

6 Country Area buses, ex Blue Bell, introduced 1930 and fitted with 1935 Weymann bodies (T346-51)

6 Country Area buses, ex Queen Line, introduced 1931 and fitted with 1935 Weymann bodies (T352-7)

4 Country Area buses, ex Amersham & District, introduced 1931 and fitted with 1935 Weymann bodies (T359/61/2/4)

1 coach, ex Watford Omnibus Co, introduced 1932 and fitted with T7/1 coach body in 1938 (T369)

1 Country Area buses, ex St Albans & District, introduced 1932 (T370)

T1 outside the Royal Forest Hotel, Chingford on the 205 to Hammond Street, the second most northerly point reached by Central Area buses (being beaten by a few hundred yards by the 84, which terminated at St Albans). A number of the original Ts were fitted with peripheral seating. *Ian Allan Library*

1   Country Area bus, ex Watford Omnibus Co,
    introduced 1930 (T371)
4   Country Area buses, ex East Surrey, introduced
    1930 (T372/3/9/88)
7   Country Area buses, ex LGOC, introduced 1929
    (T375-7/82-5)
2   coaches, ex Bucks Express, introduced 1932
    (T391/2)
1   Country Area bus, ex East Surrey, introduced 1930
    and fitted with 1935 Weymann body (T396)
50 Green Line 9T9 coaches, introduced 1936,
    which became buses in 1939 (T403-52)
266 Green Line 10T10 coaches, introduced 1938
    (T453-718)
2   Central Area buses, ex LGOC, introduced 1931
    (T1001/2)

DA class (Dennis Dart)
38 one-man buses, introduced 1930
    (DA1-22/8, 30-44)

BD class (Bedford WLB and WLG)
11 surviving Country Area buses acquired from
    independents, introduced 1931
    (BD1, 3, 7-10/5/7, 20/1/3)

LT class (AEC Renown)
199 Central Area buses, ex LGOC, introduced
    1931(LT1001-50/2-1136/8-1201)
2   Country Area buses, ex LGOC, introduced 1932
    (LT1427/8)
1   coach, ex Hillman's Saloon Coaches, introduced
    1932 (LT1429)

LTC class (AEC Renown)
24 coaches, introduced 1937 (LTC1-24)

C class (Leyland Cub)
97 one-man buses, introduced 1934 (C1-75/7-98);
8   1½-deck Inter-Station buses, introduced 1936
    (C106-13)

CR class (Leyland Cub REC)
1   one-man bus, introduced 1937 (CR1)
    *(Delivery of production CRs did not begin
    until September 1939.)*

Q class (AEC Q)
1   Central Area bus, ex LGOC, introduced 1932
    (Q1)
102 Country Area buses, introduced 1935
    (Q6-105/86/7)
80 Central and Country Area buses, introduced
    1936 (Q106-85)
50 Green Line coaches (Q189-238)

TF class (Leyland Tiger FEC)
88 Private Hire and Green Line coaches,
    introduced 1937 (TF1-88)

The interior of a Q coach
of 1936, which in a number
of features anticipated
those of both the pre- and
postwar RT. *Ian Allan Library*

DOUBLE-DECK BUSES

TD class (Leyland Titan TD1 and TD2)
108 Central and Country Area buses, acquired
from various independents, introduced 1928
(TD2, 3, 5-12/7-20/2/4/5/7-9, 34/7/8, 43/5-7,
50/2-5/7/9, 61/3/5/6/9, 79-82/9, 91/4/6/8,
103/8/12-30/3-51/4-66/70/1/3/92-5)

ST class (AEC Regent)
815 Central and Country Area buses, ex-LGOC,
East Surrey and National, introduced 1929
(ST1-135/7-9/42/56/8/61/4-836)

6 lowbridge Country Area buses, ex National,
introduced 1930 (ST136/40/1/57/62/3)

191 open-staircase Central Area buses, ex
Thomas Tilling, introduced 1930 (ST837-1027)
(Withdrawal had begun in the summer of 1939)

1 Central Area bus, ex Chariot, introduced 1930
and fitted with LT body in 1933 (ST1028)

1 Central Area bus, ex Empire, introduced 1930
and fitted with LT body in 1933 (ST1029)

1 Central Area bus, ex Pro Bono Publico,
introduced 1930 and fitted with LT body in 1933
(ST1030)

1 Central Area bus, ex Pembroke, introduced 1930
and fitted with LT body in 1933 (ST1031)

23 'Bluebird'-type Country Area buses, ex LGOC,
introduced 1932 (ST1032-9/70-84)

30 standard Country Area buses, ex LGOC,
introduced 1931 (ST1040-69)

4 Country Area buses, ex Autocar, introduced 1930
(ST1085-8)

2 lowbridge Country Area buses, ex Amersham
& District, introduced 1930 (ST1089/90)

42 standard Country Area buses, ex LGOC,
introduced 1930 (ST1091-1132)

6 Country Area buses, ex Lewis, introduced 1930
(ST1133-8)

1 Country Area bus, ex LGOC, introduced 1929
as demonstrator (ST1139)

LT class (AEC Renown)
150 open-staircase Central Area buses, ex LGOC,
introduced 1929 (LT1-150)

798 enclosed-staircase Central Area buses, ex LGOC,
introduced 1931 (LT151-740/2-949)

1 experimental Green Line coach, ex LGOC,
introduced 1931 (LT1137)

274 'Bluebird'-type Central Area buses, introduced
1931 (LT741, 950-99, 1204-1426)

ST644 stands at the Chingford terminus of the 102 alongside
a Bedford OWB normal-control single-decker — a type that
might have been foisted upon London Transport during the
war. It would certainly have been more reliable than the
rear-engined CR-class Leyland Cubs which arrived in late
1939. *Ian Allan Library*

STL class (AEC Regent)

100 Central Area buses, ex LGOC, introduced 1932 (STL1-50, 153-202)

80 Central Area buses, ex Thomas Tilling, introduced 1932 (STL51-130)

400 Central Area buses, LGOC design, introduced 1933 (STL203-552, 559-608)

5 Central Area buses, ex Pickup, introduced 1932, formerly open-top but rebuilt 1934 with Chiswick-designed tops (STL553-7)

1 open-staircase Central Area bus, ex Redline, introduced 1932 (STL558)

849 standard Central Area buses, introduced 1934 (STL609-856/8-958, 1060-1259, 1264-1463, 1514-1613)

1 experimental Central Area bus (at one time numbered STF1), introduced 1935 with full front, rebuilt as half-cab in 1938 (STL857)

139 forward-entrance Country Area buses, introduced 1935 (STL959-1043/56-9, 1464-1513)

12 forward-entrance Country Area buses with provincial-style lowbridge Weymann bodies, introduced 1934 (STL1044-55)

3 Central Area buses with ST-type bodies, introduced 1935 (STL1260/1/3)

1 Central Area bus with rebuilt Dodson body, introduced 1935 (STL1262)

994 standard roofbox Central and Country Area buses, introduced 1936 introduced 1937 (STL1614-1808/10-3/5-7/9-22/4/6/9/31-4/6-40/7/59/63/9/70/3/7-83/5-2647)

40 Central Area buses for working through the Blackwall and Rotherhithe tunnels, introduced 1937 (STL1809/14/8/23/5/7/8/30/5/41-6/8-58/60-2/4-8/71/2/4-6/84)

Q class (AEC Q)

4 Central and Country Area side-engined buses, introduced 1934 (Q2-5)

1 six-wheel Country Area bus, introduced 1937 as Green Line coach (Q188)

STD class (Leyland Titan TD4)

100 Central Area buses, introduced 1937 (STD1-100)

RT class (AEC Regent)

1 Central Area bus, introduced 1938 with temporary open-staircase body, fitted with new LT body March 1939, entered service 9 August 1939 (RT1) *(A further 338 RTs were on order.)*

123

TRAMS

1	Ex LCC 'Bluebird' (1)
1	Ex LCC rebuilt 'E/1' (2)
20	Ex East Ham Corporation (81-100)
107	Ex LCC 'HR/2' (101-59, 1854-80/2/4-1903)
101	Ex LCC 'E/3' (160, 1904-2003)
37	Ex West Ham Corporation (296-312/25-44)
25	ex Croydon Corporation (375-99)
438	Ex LCC 'E/1' (552-601, 797, 800/2/15/8-21/3/5-7/34/6/8-40/2-5/8/54/67/8/70/1/81/90/2/4/6, 904-6/13/4/6/23/4/7/31-3/6/7/40/2-4/6-66/8-82/4-96, 1000/2-42/4/9/50/3-9/61-3/6-70/2/3/5-99, 1100/1/3/7-9/12/5-9/23/4/8/37-47/9/50/2/63/5/6/70-82/4/6-91/5, 1204-6/8/9/11-20/2-52/4/5/9/60/2-8/70/3/5/7/82/4/6/8/91-4, 1302/4-6/8-10/2/3/5-8/20/2/6/8/9/32/6/8/9/43/9/71-99, 1400-26)
3	Ex LCC 'ME/3' (1370, 1441/4)
1	Ex LCC'HR/1' (1852)
1	Ex LCC 'HR/2' (1853)
20	Ex Walthamstow Corporation (2042-61)
101	Ex LCC 'Feltham' (2066-2165/7)

TROLLEYBUSES

35 'A1' AEC 663T with UCC bodywork, ex LUT, introduced 1931 (1-35)

25 'A2' AEC 663T with UCC bodywork, ex LUT, introduced 1931 (36-60)

1 'X1' AEC 691T with LGOC bodywork, ex LUT, introduced 1933 (61)

1 'X2' AEC 663T with Metro-Cammell bodywork, introduced 1934 (62)

1 'X3' AEC 661T with English Electric bodywork, introduced 1934 (63)

30 'B1' Leyland TTB2 with BRCW bodywork, introduced 1935 (64-93)

38 'B2' Leyland TTB2 with Brush bodywork, introduced 1936 (94-131)

52 'C1' AEC 664T with Weymann or Metro-Cammell bodywork, introduced 1935 (132-83)

100 'C2' AEC 664T with Metro-Cammell bodywork, introduced 1936 (184-283)

100 'C3' AEC 664T with BRCW bodywork, introduced 1936 (284-383)

1 'D1' Leyland LPTB70 with Leyland bodywork, introduced 1936 (384)

99 'D2' Leyland LPTB70 with Metro-Cammell bodywork, introduced 1936 (385-483)

5 'B3' Leyland LPTB60 with BRCW bodywork, introduced 1936 (484-8)

5 'B1' Leyland LPTB60 with BRCW bodywork, introduced 1936 (489-93)

60 'D3' Leyland LPTB70 with Leyland bodywork, introduced 1936 (494-553)

50 'E1' AEC 664T with Brush bodywork, introduced 1937 (554-603)

25 'E2' AEC 664T with Weymann bodywork, introduced 1937 (604-28)

25 'E3' AEC 664T with Park Royal bodywork, introduced 1937 (629-53)

100 'F1' Leyland LPTB70 with Leyland bodywork, introduced 1937 (654-753)

1 'X4' AEC/London Transport 'chassisless', introduced 1937 (754)

150 'H1' Leyland LPTB70 with Metro-Cammell bodywork, introduced 1938 (755-904)

48 'J1' AEC 664T with Weymann or Metro-Cammell bodywork, introduced 1938 (905-52)

1 'M1' AEC 664T with Weymann bodywork, introduced 1938 (953)

1 'L2' AEC/Metro-Cammell 'chassisless', introduced 1938 (954)

75 'J2' AEC 664T with BRCW bodywork, introduced 1938 (955-1029)

25 'J3' AEC 664T with BRCW bodywork, introduced 1938 (1030-54)

150 'K1' Leyland LPTB70 with Leyland bodywork, introduced 1938 (1055-1154, 1255-1304)

150 'K2' Leyland LPTB70 with Leyland bodywork, introduced 1938 (1155-1254, 1305-54)

15 'L1' AEC/Metro-Cammell 'chassisless', introduced 1939 (1355-69)

9 'L2' AEC/Metro-Cammell 'chassisless', introduced 1939 (1370-8)

1 'X5' AEC/Metro-Cammell 'chassisless', introduced 1939 (1379)

22 'L3' AEC/Metro-Cammell 'chassisless', introduced 1939 (1380-1401)

55 'N1' AEC 664T with BRCW bodywork, introduced 1939 (1555-93/6-1611)

11 'N2' AEC 664T with Park Royal bodywork, introduced 1939 (1645-55)

1 'X7' All-Leyland 'chassisless' demonstrator (1671)

Further trolleybuses of Classes L3, M1, N1, N2 and X6 (a 'chassisless' AEC/English Electric demonstrator) would be delivered during the remainder of 1939 and early 1940.

Left: Upper-deck interior of 'E/1' tramcar. *Author*

2: Vehicles destroyed during World War 2

Inevitably the biggest losses of LPTB vehicles occurred when garages or depots were hit. The most severe were as follows:

Two STs, 54 STLs and two Manchester Crossley Condors —58 buses in all — were destroyed at **Croydon** garage on the night of 10/11 May 1941. When the yard in Bull Lane, **Peckham**, where vehicles were stored, was hit on 22 October 1940 48 vehicles were destroyed, comprising 24 STs, 11 LTs, one C, one T and all but one of the almost new touring TF coaches (11 in all). The hit by a flying bomb on **Elmers End** garage on 18 July 1944 resulted in the destruction of 30 vehicles, 21 LTs, four STs, four STLs and one Q. Twenty-nine cars — 15 'HR2s', both 'HR1s', seven 'E3s' and five 'E1s' — were lost when **Camberwell** tram depot was hit right at the beginning of the Blitz on the night of 8 September 1940. This was followed by 16 'E1s' which were destroyed in the bombing of **Clapham** depot on 17 September 1940. The worst incident involving trolleybuses was the V1 flying-bomb raid on **Bexleyheath** depot on 19 June 1944, when 12 trolleybuses — eight 'D2s' and three 'H1s' and a 'B2' — were destroyed.

Inevitably, records of losses in such traumatic times are not wholly reliable, but below is a list of vehicles which were written off due to enemy action or accident probably related to wartime conditions (*i.e.* blackout) between 1 September 1939 and the end of the war.

The remains of what looks like an STL surrounded by devastated cars and buildings after a raid on Portman Square, 19 September 1940.
Author's collection

BUSES

ST (ex LGOC)	24, 156, 247, 500, 526, 545, 570, 600, 637, 657, 739, 788
ST (ex Tilling)	837, 839, 851, 857, 871, 879, 893, 895, 895, 896, 903, 908, 919, 923, 938, 927, 950, 956, 960,965, 967, 973, 974, 980, 990, 991, 992, 1003, 1007, 1008, 1010, 1021
LT (double-deck)	154, 172, 184, 201, 224, 254, 297, 300, 333, 363, 417, 436, 701, 732, 735, 795, 839, 849, 856
LT (single-deck)	1020, 1021, 1032, 1048, 1054, 1070, 1084, 1088, 1146, 1151, 1429
STL (original LGOC design)	2, 11, 13, 26, 32, 156, 170, 173, 174, 196
STL (ex Tilling)	53, 63, 71,82, 87, 88, 96, 97, 98, 99, 100, 101, 104, 105, 106, 107, 110, 112, 116, 120, 127, 129, 130
STL (later LGOC/ LPTB design)	302, 305, 326, 327, 388, 340, 355, 358, 364, 367, 368, 378, 380, 385, 391, 392, 393, 394, 395, 400, 402, 576
STL (ex Pickup)	554
STL (LPTB standard)	745, 782, 1288, 1386, 2046, 2184, 2250, 2418, 2424
TF	2, 3, 4, 5, 6, 7, 8, 10, 11, 12, 13

TRAMS

'E1'	597, 583, 1023, 1028, 1173, 1179, 1234, 1241, 1351, 1371, 1367, 1373, 1379, 1394, 1403, 1490, 1515, 1517, 1523, 1524, 1526, 1536, 1543, 1575, 1578, 1580, 1586, 1591, 1600, 1649, 1736, 1788, 1789, 1807, 1808, 1821, 1825, 1831, 1842
'E1/R'	826, 962, 972, 1421
'E3'	1967, 1972, 1973, 1976, 1978, 1982, 1983, 1985
'HR1'	1852, 1853
'HR2'	112, 123, 124, 129, 130, 131, 148, 1865, 1889, 1900, 1901, 1902, 1903
'ME3'	1441
Ex Croydon	396
Ex Walthamstow	2044, 2051
'Feltham'	2109, 2113

TROLLEYBUSES

'B2'	99
'C3'	364
'D2'	386, 387, 394, 398, 412, 428, 435, 448
'H1'	787, 791, 812
'L1'	1365
'L3'	1387
'M1'	953

In addition 9T9 T443 and 10T10 Ts 460, 486, 488, 509, 578, 586, 587, 594, 665, 666, 670, 681 did not return from service with the American military or Red Cross.

There were also a large number of buses and trolleybuses whose chassis survived enemy action and were fitted with replacement bodies, as well as at least three examples of buses which were more or less destroyed but whose identities were perpetuated, the vehicles being reconstructed from spare parts.

The remains of a trolleybus after a raid on Holloway on 17 October 1940.
London Transport Museum

3: The survivors, 2010

This section does *not* attempt to list all London Transport buses, trams and trolleybuses which were at work either throughout the 1939-45 war or for some part of it and are still in existence but rather those which are most accessible within the UK and are likely to be seen in museums or at rallies. There are a great many more which are officially still in existence, although some may actually be deceased, and others which are inaccessible to the public or exist only in chassis form or are so derelict as to be beyond all reasonable hope of resuscitation. It does not include vehicles which were preserved before 1939.

BUSES

T31 (UU 6646)

One of the great survivors. One of the LGOC's very first batch of AEC Regal buses, T31 entered service from Nunhead garage on 31 December 1929. It moved around, Cricklewood, Tottenham and West Green garages being amongst its homes in the 1930s. Quite early on it was converted from rear- to forward-entrance and continued at work in this form right through the war years. It was withdrawn in July 1948 but reprieved and continued its nomadic existence, working from Kingston — inevitably — Sidcup and Mortlake garages. In June 1950 its petrol engine was replaced by a diesel and although many of its contemporaries were either being withdrawn or rebuilt by Marshall it continued in passenger service until July 1952 when, at the age of 22½ — making it just about the longest-serving London bus and the last ex-LGOC in service — it became a trainer from Hounslow. Remarkably it continued on these duties until June 1956, by which time it was living at Norbiton. Its remarkable longevity had not gone unnoticed, and the well-known writer and authority on London buses, Ken Blacker, and a group of friends including Prince Marshall and Michael Dryhurst, bought it for £45. This is generally accepted as the beginning of the private bus-preservation movement. T31 was stored at Swiss Cottage and the preservationists discovered that, hardly surprisingly, it needed a great deal of tender, loving care. This it received over the years. Eventually, in 1979, it reappeared exactly as it had

been on the last day of December 1929, looking utterly magnificent in the short-lived experimental LGOC livery of red, pale-yellow waistrail and window frames, silver roof with a black strip dividing it from the windows and black mudguards. Bought with the assistance of a 50% grant from the Science Museum, it came to Cobham Bus Museum in June 1994 and is often seen out on the road.

T219c (GK 5486)

One of the original Green Line AEC Regals (chassis No 662715), fitted with a 30-seat, forward-entrance, Chiswick-designed Duple body dating from January 1931. Originally totalling 250 these Regals were withdrawn from Green Line work in 1938/9, being replaced largely by the 10T10 Regals; many were sold, others converted to service vehicles and some downgraded to buses. On the outbreak of war T219 was one of 16 converted to staff ambulances, fitted with bunks and first-aid kits and renumbered 428W. It was painted olive green and sent to Hendon garage. Hardly used, fortunately, during the war years, it was restored to passenger service afterwards, serving as a Country Area bus at Windsor, and ended its working days in the Central Area in 1950. London Transport decided to restore an early T to its original Green Line condition and livery and T219, being the one in best condition, was chosen. Stored at Reigate garage, it first went on public display at Clapham Museum, then Syon Park, later dividing its time between Covent Garden and Acton. Every so often it is let out of captivity and can be seen out on the road on such occasions as the Historic Commercial Vehicle Society London to Brighton run on the first Sunday in May.

T357 (GN 8242)

One of the most interesting of all surviving vintage London vehicles, T357 has a unique history both during its LPTB ownership and afterwards. There were more permutations and varieties of T than any other London bus, the only commonality being that they were all AEC Regals. T357 perfectly illustrates this all on its own. Although its present body was built by Weymann in 1935, it previously had one built by the unprepossessing-sounding London Lorries, which was actually the predecessor of Park Royal, dating from March 1931

when it was delivered to Queen Line coaches of Baldock. A companion, T369, which was also rebodied, a little later, in 1936, had actually begun its career as demonstrator in Peru(!) in 1930. T357 now classified 5T4 with its new, all-metal body, worked initially as a 26-seat Green Line coach, and was altered to a 30-seat bus in 1938. During the war, in December 1942, T357 was altered to work on producer gas being converted back in the late summer of 1944. By this date it had been painted grey as it was working from Addlestone garage on

route 462 which served the Vickers aircraft works. This included none other than outstation W45 (currently Cobham Bus Museum), where T357 lives. In May 1945 T357 was one of a number of T- and C-class vehicles sold to the Allied Control Commission in Germany, later passing to an owner in northern France. After spending decades in a barn near Dunkirk it was brought home and arrived at Cobham Bus Museum on 14 March 2003. It is hoped restoration will begin shortly.

The rear aspect of T31, including the stage-carriage registration plate required by the Metropolitan Police. *Author*

T448 (CXX 171)

The only surviving example of 50 9T9 Green Line coaches built in 1936, T448 took up work from Hitchin garage in June 1936 working routes K1 and K2. However, the 3hr 36min journey between Hitchin and Dorking proved too demanding for the 7.7-litre engine, and T448, along with the other 9T9s, was relegated some two years later to bus work. It served as an ambulance in the Hammersmith area during the war and was restored to bus work in 1946, operating from Leatherhead, Addlestone, Guildford and, finally, in 1952, Central Area Kingston, although it retained green livery. Next it performed staff transport duties between Reigate garage and Chiswick Works, before being sold to Harperbury Hospital at St Albans. Engine failure in 1958 meant what looked like the end for T448, for it was sold to scrap dealers, first Marlboro of St Albans in 1960 and then later that year to Watling Street Motors of Redbourne. However, it survived and was sold on in 1968 to preservationists who ran it on the HCVC run to Brighton and elsewhere. Now at Cobham Museum, it awaits overhaul.

T499 (ELP 223)

For the best part of 20 years it was assumed that just one of the classic 10T10s, T504, had survived (see below). Then in the late 1990s rumours began to circulate that one other had been found in Australia. Australian preservationist Ian Kerr followed up these rumours and did indeed discover what turned out to be T499 on a farm 370km south of Perth. Although understandably in rather less than pristine condition and with its front wheels and seats missing, it was nevertheless far more complete than might have been expected. New in the summer of 1938, T499 had entered Green Line service from Grays garage on 1 July that year, moved on to Watford, then Hatfield before conversion to an ambulance on the outbreak of war. It returned to its intended role from Windsor on 1 March 1946 and continued in Green Line service until withdrawn from Staines garage in September 1953. Its sale in April 1954 to Leeds-based bus dealer W. North triggered the chain of events which would see it become an Australian citizen for over 50 years. Tony Creasey, who operated a school bus service in Western Australia asked his father in the UK to look for a suitable second-hand vehicle. T499 was chosen, for which North's was paid £250; the cost of shipping it was

T448 leads RTL358 southbound towards Brighton for a rally. *Author*

£Australian 500, plus another £Australian 500 import duty, and it worked as a school bus between Kendenup and Mt Barker for some five years. Sold on for further service, it eventually went into a retirement which would last over 40 years. On 24 November 1997 it arrived on a low loader at the Bus Museum of Western Australia. Tony had originally intended to carry out restoration himself, but in 2005 he sold it to Ensign, and in November that year it came back to England ready for restoration to begin and a resumption of service in London.

T504 (ELP 228)

This is the other surviving example of the ultimate front-engined Green Line Regal, the 10T10, of which 266 were built in 1938/9. A development of the 9T9, the 10T10 abandoned the rather clumsy built-up frontal appearance and bumper and boasted an 8.8-litre diesel engine which proved ideal for Green Line work. T504 entered service in May 1938 on routes E (Aylesbury–Chelsham) and F (Hemel Hempstead–Tatsfield/Edenbridge). Official documents give its allocation as Staines (ST), but this cannot be accurate, as Staines is a very long way from routes E and F. In September 1939 T504 became an ambulance. It returned to Green Line work in 1946 — a welcome indication that peacetime normality was returning. Replaced by RFs in 1951, a number of 10T10s, including T504, were repainted in red livery, had their doors permanently sealed open, and worked from Sidcup garage until 1954. Sold in 1954 to well-known Yorkshire dealer W. North, T504 suffered the indignity of being shunted around various dealers

until it was discovered in a scrapyard in Oldham, and on 28 December 1968 began its journey into restoration. Despite broken cab windows a group of brave souls towed it all the way from Lancashire through the bitterly cold night of 28/29 December to Essex. Although the vehicle was now safe, the

group of enthusiasts had their hands full working on RT113 and reluctantly sold T504 in November 1976 to Cobham Bus Museum. Restoration followed fairly rapidly and the Green Line coach made its first public appearance in preservation at the 150 Years of London Buses Rally in July 1979.

Above and right: **T504** enters and leaves Wisley airfield before and after 2010's edition of the Cobham bus rally. *Author*

LT1059 (GO 5170)

One of two surviving single-deck LT Renowns (nicknamed 'Scooters'), a 1LTL1 with Chiswick-built 35-seat, forward-entrance bodywork, placed in service in May 1931. These were the most numerous type of LPTB Central Area single-decker throughout the 1930s and the war years. Eleven, plus a former Hillmans coach, were written off as a result of enemy action, but the class otherwise remained intact until withdrawal began at the end of 1948 with the arrival of the TD class. LT1059 was withdrawn on 8 September 1949. After passing through various hands it was discovered in use as a holidaymakers' bicycle store in Teignmouth in 1970, although, it was apparently still able to move under its own power, and attempts were made to preserve it at Cobham. These came to nothing, but more than two decades later, in March 1994, it was bought (for £2,000) by two London Bus Preservation Trust members at an auction at a farm at Offham, Kent, and finally brought to Cobham, where it awaits restoration.

LT1076 (GO 5198)

The second surviving single-deck LT, like LT1059 new in May 1931. Although 60 of the class were rebuilt by Marshall in 1948/9, neither of the preserved examples received this treatment. LT1076 was allocated to Dalston, Leyton and Elmers End garages, being withdrawn from the latter, where it worked the 227, on 27 June 1950. The class, both rebuilt examples and those in original condition, had disappeared by the end of 1953 after serving the capital and its suburbs for 22 years. In those days bus preservation by individuals had barely begun and London Transport did not see fit to preserve a single-deck LT. However, LT1076 was not broken up and for a time served as a summer house at High Wycombe. Eventually, like LT1059, it was offered for sale, woebegone but fairly intact and with a quantity of spares, in 1994. Having got a second chance the London Transport Museum was not going to miss out this time and bought it for £1,200, having already put £60,000 aside for its restoration, the money coming both from the Friends of the LT Museum and the Science Museum Prism Fund. This it did and LT1076 made its first official public appearance on the HCVC run to Brighton in May 2005 looking absolutely stunning in mid-1930s condition. It won outright the National Benzole Concours d'Elégance award, as well as several others.

LT165 speeds away from the camera while on its way to Brighton. *Author*

LT165 (GK 5323)

The only surviving double-deck London Transport Renown, this impressive six-wheel example entered service in 1930. It originally had a standard, enclosed 56-seat body with, like its 350 identical brothers, a single indicator at the front for destination, via points and number. Later it was fitted with an LT5 body, which it retains today. This has a rather stylish inward slope to the upper deck and an indicator box mounted above the cab roof. This gave the destination and number and above that was a via board, illuminated by a lamp hung from the upper-deck front windows. Having never seen this in operation, such frills being discarded in wartime, we wartime bus spotters were quite unable to fathom its purpose and had to wait for the first Ian Allan *'ABC'* to enlighten us. Many regret that London Transport did not choose to preserve one of the original LTs, which, despite their open staircases, are entitled to be described as the first really modern London double-deckers. Prince Marshall, that pioneer preservationist to whom we owe so much, seemingly had plans to get hold of a Renown chassis and build a replica original LT body on it, but sadly he died before he could set the project in motion. Nevertheless, LT165 serves as a fine representative of its class.

ST821 (GK 3192)

The standard ST entered service in 1930, a few months after the first LTs and was a shorter, Regent version, of the LT. ST821 is fitted with an LGOC 48-seat ST9 body and took up service with the National Omnibus and Transport Company, a wholly owned LGOC subsidiary, in March 1931 at Ware garage. Unlike its Metropolitan sisters it was fitted with a windscreen and a door from the outset and had a slightly smaller front indicator. It later moved south to Dorking, then back north to Hertford, briefly after the war to Windsor and ended passenger service at Watford in May 1949. Presumably being in better condition than its compatriots it entered the museum collection at Reigate garage in January 1950 and the curious decision was taken to paint it red, a colour it had never worn. It lost its door at some point in its career, but its front indicator gave away the game that it had never been a Central Area bus. By the time it had moved to Covent Garden it had been repainted into its final, correct, green and white Country Area livery.

ST922 (GJ 2098)

In 1930/1 the Thomas Tilling company mounted its own design of bodywork on 191 examples of the AEC Regent chassis. When these entered the LPTB fleet they were given the numbers ST837-1027. Throughout the 1930s they remained at the former Tilling garages of Croydon, Bromley and Catford. The first examples were withdrawn just before the outbreak of war but none was broken up and all, except for damaged vehicles, lasted until 1945. ST922, which had begun work from Bromley garage in June 1930, later moved to Catford then, from August to December 1940, served at the southernmost tip of LT's empire as a guardroom at Tunbridge Wells garage. From December 1941 to November 1944 it was loaned to Midland Red, thus qualifying, one hopes, for a guest appearance one day at Wythall museum, then came back to finish passenger work in London at Putney (AF) garage, where it would not have compared very favourably with the vastly more modern 'prewar' RTs. Withdrawn in April 1947, London Transport nevertheless still had a use for it, converting it, along with five other Tillings, to a mobile canteen, No 693J, replacing an NS. British Road Services bought it in May 1955 and some 10 years later it had the great good luck to be spotted by Prince Marshall in the scrapyard of Rush Green Motors. Despite being told that it was beyond resuscitation, he bought it in December 1966 and had it restored so splendidly that we were able to ride on it on sightseeing service 100 through Central London from Covent Garden Museum in the early 1970s. Now resident at Cobham Museum, it is a familiar sight at rallies and was the oldest bus to take part in the commemorative runs on the 159 route on 8 December 2005 to mark the end of ordinary Routemaster operation in London.

ST922 *en route* to Brighton. *Author*

Breakdown tender 738J derives from STL169 and is seen at the outer edge of Wisley airfield during the Cobham rally of 2010. *Author*

STL169 (AGX 520), latterly van 738J

The STL was a 1ft-longer version of the Regent ST chassis. AGX 520 began its career as STL169, one of the original, extremely boxy-looking LGOC 60-seat members of the class, in June 1933. In January 1950 Chalmers of Redhill fitted the chassis with an Underground breakdown-tender body. However, the vehicle's bus origins remained obvious, for it retained an STL half cab front end; the only thing was that it looked just like one belonging to a standard LPTB STL rather than that of STL169! No-one seems to know why Chalmers went to this length rather than retain the existing cab. As 738J it worked until February 1971 and is now preserved at Cobham Bus Museum.

STL390 (AXM 649), latterly van 830J

Identical to 738J, this was once STL390, one of the sloping-front STL3 variety, dating from April 1934. It too was converted by Chalmers, in March 1950. It can now be seen at Acton, being part of the London Transport Museum collection.

STL441 (AXM 693)

From the same batch of buses as STL390, STL441 remains a bus. It entered service from Chalk Farm garage in June 1934. A very modern-looking bus for its time, it had not yet quite achieved the classic appearance of its immediate successors, which looked much the same from the sides and back but had a sloping front. STL441 originally had a 7.7-litre petrol engine but, during overhaul at Chiswick Works in May 1939, this was replaced by a flexibly mounted 7.7-litre diesel engine and a pre-selector gearbox. This caused it to be raised slightly at the front; from then on all this group of buses so fitted were known as the 'sit up and beg' variety. Like so many LPTB buses by the end of the war its body was in a sorry state and so it was sent off to Mann Egerton of Cambridge in January 1948 for an extensive rebuild. This ensured its survival until September 1952, latterly working from Streatham (AK) garage which retained large numbers of the STLs well into the RT era. Several STLs were at this time being exported to mainland Europe for their scrap value, but although this was its destination too STL441 was vastly more fortunate, finding a place at a museum in the Netherlands, to be precise Het National Automobielmuseum at Leidschendam in The Hague. Eventually it was replaced by an RTL and returned home, to the Cobham Bus Museum in August 1974. Recently it has undergone an extensive restoration and its appearance now is exactly as it would have been in 1948 on its return from rebuilding by Mann Egerton.

Above and left: The wretched weather encountered at Wisley on 6 April 2008 almost threatened to see Cobham called off that year, but STLs 441 and 2377 proved more than equal to the task. *Author*

Right: STL2692, the only survivor of the non-standard Daimler, Leyland and AEC buses bought by London Transport between 1945 and the arrival of the first postwar RTs in 1947. It is seen at the Carlton Colville Museum, Lowestoft, that extraordinary haven of London buses, trolleybuses and trams deep in East Anglia, during the London Transport 70th-anniversary celebrations in 2003. Next to it is 938J, a recovery vehicle converted shortly after the war from STL169. *Author*

STL469 (AYV 651)

Originally identical to STL441, STL469 entered service on 24 July 1934, one of no fewer than 22 STLs sent new that month to Chalk Farm garage. Like STL441, it was fitted with a diesel engine just before the war, at a cost of £425, but it was reckoned that the reduced fuel consumption would mean a saving of £266 per year. As STL469 worked on right through the 1940s and into the 1950s, not being withdrawn until the first day of January 1954, London Transport certainly made the right decision. Like the London Transport Collection's ST and LT, this example of the STL was hardly the most obvious choice, which would surely have been one of the final, roofbox-number version. However, it was STL469 which was the lucky vehicle. It had been a Central Area vehicle all its life except for a final few months working from Dartford garage, but it retained red livery. Like the preserved ST, it was given a livery in preservation which it had never worn, that is with cream upper-deck window frames. Indeed, none of this particular variety of STL was ever painted in this livery after overhaul, although a few did subsequently receive it so it could be claimed to be authentic for the type. Never rebuilt after the war, it ended its days in all-over red apart from a cream waistband and this is how it is now presented.

STL1470 (CXX 457), latterly 971J

This started out as a Country Area forward-entrance bus, delivered to Dorking garage in December 1936. Taken out of service, briefly, on the outbreak of war, it was soon back at work and continued to serve in the various varieties of London Transport green until withdrawal from passenger service. In March 1953 it had its upper-deck windows and roof removed, becoming one of five STLs converted for tree-lopping. As such, painted in Chiswick service green, a rather drab colour which gave it the air of something belonging to the War Department, it worked all over the leafier parts of the London Transport empire, which was as likely to be Kennington High Road as the slopes of the Chilterns or the North Downs, until September 1963 when it was replaced by a purpose-built Thames Trader. The STLs were the last generation of buses to continue with London Transport after conversion to service vehicles. Sold to a preservationist who used it as a caravan, the former STL1470 later passed into the hands of Messrs Stubbington and Peters, who did an

excellent job in carefully turning it out exactly as it had been in its tree-lopping days, even to the extent of appearing at rallies complete with shears and tree branches! It now belongs to the London Bus Company of Rainham and may eventually be restored as a Country Area bus.

STL2093 (DLU 92)

An example of *the* classic prewar London bus, the final version of its type with the roof-mounted route-number box. In March 1955 STL2093 was acquired by Mr D. Cowing from Reliance Motor Services of Newbury, which had run it for several years after withdrawal by London Transport, and, even if the restoration to prewar livery was not 100% authentic, inasmuch as it had a 1939-vintage body removed from the chassis of an STL which was to be converted to an SRT in 1949 (its own chassis dating from June 1937) and there were a few other, minor postwar modifications, it nevertheless looked superb. Having been rallied for a number of years, it eventually arrived at Cobham Bus Museum in August 1984 and at the time of writing is undergoing a complete restoration courtesy of Ensign. Summing up everything that makes the restoration of bygone buses and coaches such a a delight, STL2093 has also been the inspiration for numerous model versions, most notably that produced by Dinky Toys.

STL2377 (EGO 426)

The other surviving roofbox STL, this is in many enthusiasts' eyes the gem of the Cobham collection. Delivered in November 1937 to Holloway (J) garage, it served at a number of Central Area garages, its last one being Hornchurch (RD) from where it was withdrawn in December 1953. Like STL2093, it has survived on account of finding another owner, Mulley's Motorways Ltd of Ixworth, Suffolk, which kept it in passenger service until November 1961. The STL was the first class of London double-decker to continue with PSV work after their London days were over in any significant numbers. It was bought for preservation in 1966. It came, uncompleted, to Cobham in March 1988 and, with the assistance of a large grant from the Science Museum Prism Fund, it finally appeared in public in 2000 in the condition it would have been after its first overhaul just before the outbreak of war. The most perfect restoration job imaginable, it looks quite glorious complete with authentic advertisements with which London

The elegant lines of STL2377 are clear in this Redhill Road view taken outside Cobham Bus Museum. *Author*

buses have always been plentifully adorned and a range of destination blinds and is invariably the star of any show at which it appears.

Q55 (BXD 576)

Introduced in September 1935, this was a revolutionary Country Area vehicle with BRCW bodywork, classified 4Q4. A side-engine layout allowed for 37 passengers, with two sitting beside the driver, although the latter was later given a full-width cab and the seating capacity reduced to 35. During the war, it was converted to standee layout with seats arranged around the perimeter, allowing space for 20 standing passengers. Withdrawn in 1953, it became part of the official London Transport Collection.

Q83 (CGJ 188)

New in October 1935 and identical to Q55, this Country Area bus was converted for Green Line service in 1937 and ran from Leatherhead and Watford, Leavesden Road garages. The arrival of the 10T10s saw it revert to Country Area bus work at Guildford, then Windsor and, from 1943 to 1949, St Albans. It was taken out of service from Reigate garage in May 1953 and sold for use as an old people's ambulance. It was bought for preservation in 1966 by Bill Cottrell, one of the founder members of the London Bus Preservation Group, and took up residence at Cobham Bus Museum. Bill donated it to the museum shortly before his sad and untimely death. It has been repainted in red, as a number of these Qs worked for a time in the Central Area.

The Q class of single-and double-deckers allowed experimentation with the engine position; the side-engined configuration allowed a lower step entry and level floor. *Author*

C4 (BXD 628)

As AEC did not produce a suitable, small, normal-control bus London Transport decided that when the time came to replace the LGOC Dennis Darts the Leyland Cub would fit the role. C4 entered service in April 1935 from Addlestone garage. In June 1938 it moved to Chelsham, where it spent the rest of its London Transport career. Withdrawn in October 1953 and replaced by a GS, it was sold to A G Linfield. In March 2007 it was acquired for preservation by Ensign.

C94 (CLE 122)

Delivered in May 1936 to Enfield garage, C94 was transferred to Old Kent Road in 1940 before moving to Northfleet in 1945. It was sold in September 1954; decades later it was restored to Central Area livery and in 1993 joined the London Transport Collection.

RT1 (EYK 396)

Strictly speaking it is only the body which can call itself RT1, the chassis being originally that of Cravens-bodied postwar RT1420. RT1 began work from Chelverton Road, Putney, on route 22 on 17 July 1939. It served throughout the war but at the end of it RT1 as such disappeared, the chassis being withdrawn in late 1945 and broken up in the new year, whilst the body was transferred to RT19.

RT19 ended passenger service in 1954 and the body again parted company with its chassis, this time moving on to that of SRT45, which, in a previous life, had, before modification, belonged to STL2551. The two were now identified as Instruction Unit 1019J but seem to have been incompatible and a divorce was arranged, the somewhat promiscuous RT1 body now pairing up with Cravens RT1420, its own body having come off worse in an altercation with a low railway bridge. Clearly RT1's body had now found its soulmate, for the two have been together for 53 years. Identified in the service fleet as 1037J, the bus was eventually set aside and bought by Prince Marshall in 1978. Very few knew quite what was happening, which made RT1's re-appearance in all its original 1939 glory at Barking all the more dramatic on the last day of RT operation on 7 April 1979. The sad death of Prince Marshall saw his collection broken up and RT1 exported to the USA. Many were appalled by this, and a campaign led by equally well known preservationist, writer and photographer Michael Dryhurst, happily very much still with us, brought back RT1 in September 1986. Eventually a very expensive and very thorough overhaul was completed in time for RT1 to appear at the 2009 Cobham Bus Rally, where a successful appeal was launched to raise the funds to keep it in the UK.

Compare the steady evolution of London Transport bus design as RT1 stands beside STL441, five years its senior. *Author*

RT8 (FXT 183)

This bus entered service on 25 February 1940 from Chelverton Road, Putney (AF). The first 'prewar' RT to be preserved, it was shipped to the National Museum of Transport, St Louis, USA, in November 1961. Repatriated in 2006, it has since been superbly restored by Ensignbus, of Purfleet.

RT44 (FXT 219)

Also entering service Chelverton Road, Putney (AF) on 2 January 1940, RT44 later worked from Putney Bridge (F) garage, before returning to AF, where it ended passenger service in 1955. In use as a staff bus and training vehicle at Hendon garage (AE) until 1962, it was sold in 1963, and bought for preservation by E. H. Brakell from J. Hardwick, 1964. It is presently owned by Mr R. Wood of Marchwood.

Above: The rear end of the restored RT8, complete with wartime advertisement. *Author*

Below: Resplendent in wartime livery, RT8 made its debut in August 2010 after four years of painstaking restoration, literally from the ground up. It. *Author*

The only surviving London Transport austerity bus of the 435 built to wartime specifications, G351, a Park Royal-bodied Guy Arab of 1945. Sold in 1952, it was acquired by Burton-on-Trent Corporation, which in turn sold it in June 1967 to the Rev John Lines, who cancelled his life insurance to pay for it! When inspected the bus had no engine and the wrong radiator, so when a similar vehicle with the correct radiator came into the garage off service a mechanic exchanged radiators; a correct Gardner engine was obtained from scrap dealer W. North, possibly from a Scottish SMT Guy which it had bought from London Transport. John could not afford a full set of roadworthy tyres, so some almost bald ones were fitted which got him back to London. After several restorations it is now resident at Cobham Bus Museum and is seen after the 2006 HCVS run to Brighton. *Author*

Although this looks like a detail of lowbridge D130, complete with period passenger, it is actually an almost identical preserved bus delivered to Huddersfield Corporation in 1944, in disguise and seen at Winchester on 1 January 2008. *Author*

RT54 (FXT 229)

Entering service on 12 January 1940, this bus was withdrawn and sold to Smiths of Reading in June 1956. In 1967, it was bought for preservation by Alan Farrow, sold on several times, and is presently with R.Wood of Marchwood.

RT113 (FXT 288)

This bus entered service on 7 March 1940 at Putney Bridge garage. Ending its passenger service in 1955, it became a trainer and staff bus at Shepherd's Bush garage until 1963. It was sold on 1 May 1963 to the 2RT2 Preservation Group for £105, and appeared at the 150 Years of London Buses rally in Hyde Park on 8 July 1979. Still owned by the group, it is the 'prewar' RT most often seen at rallies.

G351 (HGC 130)

It might be argued this bus has no place in this list, as it did not enter service until February 1946, six months after World War 2 ended. However, it is the only surviving complete, authentic example of an austerity wartime design and must surely be included. A Guy Arab II with Park Royal body, it served its entire London career at Upton Park garage. Withdrawn in 1952 and stored until April 1953, it was sold to W. North, which in November 1953 sold it on to Burton Corporation, one of six ex-London Guys which served with this operator. Withdrawn by Burton in January 1967, after a very long working life for a 'wartime' bus, it was bought for preservation by the Rev John Lines and now resides at Cobham Bus Museum.

TRAMS

No 1

Introduced by the London County Council in 1932, this was intended to be the prototype of a wonderful new fleet, but with the absorption of the LCC into London Transport in 1933, it was made clear the tram network was doomed and thus No 1 remained unique. Originally allocated to Holloway depot, it moved south to Telford Avenue where it spent the rest of its London career. It did little work, usually only appearing at rush hour — your author once travelled on it coming home from school — and it was sold to Leeds in 1951. When the Leeds system closed in 1959 it became part of the London Transport Collection. It is presently at the National Tramway Museum, Crich, awaiting restoration.

No 106

This tram entered service as a B-type open-top, four-wheeled car in 1906. It was converted in 1927 to a snowbroom, No 022. Largely at the instigation of Richard Elliott, an engineer at Charlton Works, London Transport decided to preserve it when the system closed. The London County Council Tramways Trust was set up to restore it to its original condition, and this it did. No 106 can nowadays be sampled at Crich.

No 1025

An example of London's 'standard' car, the 'E1' class, introduced in 1907 as a development of the previous year's 'E'-class bogie design. Production continued (for far too long!) until 1930 and eventually totalled exactly 1,000. The body of No 1025 was built at the LCC's Charlton works in 1907 and fitted with Hurst Nelson trucks. Modernised 'Pullmanised' was the official, misleading term) in the late 1920s, 1025 worked until April 1952 when it was set aside for preservation as part of the London Transport Collection.

No 1622

A remarkable survivor, this 'E1/R' was stored throughout the war in Hampstead depot, then sold for use as a holiday home at Hayling Island in 1946. Eventually its remains were rescued by members of the LCC Tramways Trust and after much painstaking research and detailed work it emerged in the late 1990s as one of the 154 rehabilitated cars which were improved in the late 1930s and today can be admired and ridden upon at Crich.

No 1858

Numbering 109 cars, the 'HR2' class, built by the LCC in 1930, was a development of the previous year's 'HR1' and was designed for working hilly routes and fitted with EMB equal-wheel trucks with roller bearings. Their bodies, a modernised version of the 'E1', were identical to that of the contemporary 'E3' class. Many of the 'HR2s' survived to the end of the first generation of London trams on 5 July 1952. No 1858 was bought and put on display at the entrance to Chessington Zoo, where it managed to survive the elements and vandalism. Eventually it was brought to the East Anglian Transport Museum at Carlton Colville, near Lowestoft, and restored to working order, a long way from home, but a Mecca for London tram and trolleybus *aficionadi*, not least through the efforts of that authority on all things appertaining to LT history, Ken Blacker.

Above: 'HR2' No 1858 is resplendent at Carlton Colville. *Author*

Left: 'HR2' No 1858 beside 'C2' trolleybus No 260. *Author*

Beautifully restored centre-entrance 'Feltham' No 331 at Crich. *Author*

No 2099

The 100 'Felthams', built by the Union Construction Co of Feltham, Middlesex, were quite simply the finest modes of street transport anyone in London had ever come across when they were introduced jointly by the Metropolitan Electric Tramways and the London United Tramways in 1930/1. Enormously long (40ft 6in over fenders), seating 64 passengers in great comfort, with room for 10 standing passengers, the driver seated in a totally enclosed cab, their bodies were built of steel and aluminium. They were mounted on two EMB maximum-traction trucks. They instantly made every other tram look old-fashioned and even the Leyland Titan and the AEC Regent stopped sneering and realised that they had now got serious competition on their hands. Sadly, of course, it was all too late. Within a few short years they had been displaced from their intended routes in North and West London by trolleybuses, which was your author's good fortune, for they migrated south of the river to Telford Avenue and enabled him to travel on them to and from school and up to London. One was destroyed in 1940, and two more, Nos 2109 and 2113, by flying bombs in 1944, but nearly all migrated to Leeds in 1951. When that system closed No 2099 became part of the London Transport Collection.

No 2166

One of three prototype 'Felthams', this car, as No 331, was designed with a central entrance and entered service with the MET in June 1930. Because it couldn't be fitted with ploughs for conduit working it was not transferred to Telford Avenue but sold in 1937 to Sunderland Corporation. This ensured its survival for when that system closed the tram preservation movement, which would eventually set up home in a quarry in the Peak District, was getting under way and No 331 was bought for preservation. Today it is one of the gems of the Crich collection and despite its centre entrance is in all other respects a standard 'Feltham', a delight to ride on and perfectly illustrates how far ahead of its time was the 'Feltham' design.

TROLLEYBUSES

No 1 (HX 2756)

The first of the 'Diddlers' — no-one seems to know how the nickname originated. An AEC 663T with UCC bodywork, it entered service in May 1931 with London United Tramways, based at Fulwell depot, with its 59 companions, marking the beginning of the end of the original London tram system. Not surprisingly No 1 bears some resemblance to the contemporary 'Feltham' tram, although it lacks that vehicle's elegance and fine proportions. Nevertheless, it was vastly more comfortable than the elderly trams it replaced and was the forerunner of what would become the largest trolleybus fleet in the world. Not the most substantially built of vehicles, the 'Diddlers' were worn out by 1945, and orders were put in place for replacements. The first of the magnificent 'Q1s' arrived in 1948, and No 1 was withdrawn and entered the London Transport collection. It reappeared on the streets of Kingston, which it knew so well, on the final day of London's trolleybuses, 8 May 1962. Today it can usually be found at Acton.